Killing By Proxy

Alan Stewart is a retired Tayside Police inspector who, after 6 hours' retirement in 1997, went on to be the force wildlife crime officer in a civilian capacity, the first full-time post in Scotland. His interest in wildlife crime stemmed from dealing with salmon and deer poaching cases early in his career, and from an interest in farming, shooting, fishing and the countryside in general. Retiring from this role in 2011, he continued wildlife crime-related work as an intelligence officer with the UK National Wildlife Crime Unit, finally retiring in 2015. Alan was presented with several prestigious awards during his policing career, including in 2001 the MBE for services to policing wildlife crime and is the author of four books on that subject. He lives with his wife, dog, ducks and hens on the edge of a Perthshire village.

Killing By Proxy

Wildlife Crime in the UK Today

ALAN STEWART

For Clive

Hope this book helps with awareness-raising of the worst of our wildlife crimes.

Alan Stewart

Dec 2017

THIRSTY
BOOKS
EDINBURGH

Published in 2017 by Thirsty Books, Edinburgh
thirstybooks.com

ISBN: 978-0-9932828-4-3

The author's right to be identified as author of this book
under the Copyright, Designs and Patents Act 1988 has been asserted.
The paper used in this book is recyclable. It is made from low chlorine pulps
produced in a low energy, low emission manner from renewable forests.

Printed and bound by Bell & Bain Ltd., Glasgow

Typeset by Main Point Books, Edinburgh
© Alan Stewart 2017

Contents

For the staff, past and present, of the UK National Wildlife Crime Unit. Working with this most professional unit was both a privilege and a pleasure.

INTRODUCTION

This book captures and analyses some of the most prominent wildlife crimes reported over the past four years or so in the media, including social media. The media plays a pivotal role in informing the general public about the shocking events that are regular occurrences in some parts of the countryside, and in raising awareness of the difficulties the police face in the investigation of wildlife crime.

Some of those commenting on wildlife incidents have no great grasp of the law, or the difficulties involved in detecting and prosecuting wrongdoers. More significantly, depending on the commentator, some media responses are clearly skewed in favour of vested interests such as landowners and the shooting and hunting fraternity. Others exhibit an unfair bias against these country pursuits without due consideration of those in the industry who are doing their best for the environment and its wildlife, and staying within the law while doing so.

I have been involved with the media on almost all aspects of wildlife crime for many years. As far back as the late 1960s I was quoted in the press while still a uniformed police constable dealing with deer and salmon poaching cases. Much later, from 1993 and as the force wildlife crime officer for the then Tayside Police, I began to write articles for newspapers and magazines on a wide variety of wildlife crime, especially in advance of seasonal wildlife crime trends such as hare coursing, wild bird egg theft and poisoning of raptors. This continued right through my 18 years in this role and also into my three years as intelligence officer with the UK National Wildlife Crime Unit (NWCU). The NWCU role was invaluable in that it gave me an insight into wildlife crime over the whole of the United Kingdom.

My links with the media also included involvement with the BBC 2 series *Wildlife Detectives* which, over the course of a year, filmed a series of wildlife crime investigations in Scotland as they occurred. I assisted a German film crew making a film on deer poaching in Scotland and an American film crew creating the much-acclaimed documentary on wild bird egg thieving, appropriately entitled *Poached*. My career in the policing of wildlife crime unfortunately terminated through illness in January 2015. Since then I have continued my interest in wildlife crime through my blog wildlifedetective.wordpress.com.

Until the point that there is a conviction, the police are ultra-cautious in naming estates that are very clearly involved in wildlife crime. Formerly, I ran almost all my articles and draft press releases through the force communications staff before publication or submission to the media and they normally edited it to a bare minimum. A media release will nearly always state that a particular incident, for instance the recovery of a poisoned bait, took place in an area of a county rather than on a particular estate. Even though the recovery is a fact and not an accusation against an individual, and even if there have been countless similar incidents discovered on that estate, it will not be named. This frustrated me and seemed not to be in the public interest. Hot on the heels of the press release I was usually contacted by various reporters – and very often by radio and television – but my comments to expand the press release had to be in line with the force policy.

Writing this book I have thoroughly enjoyed not having fretful media relations staff looking over my shoulder, and I hope what follows is the better for not having had their interference. Though I have to be cognisant of libel, I am much less constrained now that I have retired and can reveal more information on issues that are not sub judice. After half a century of dealing with wildlife crime I can at last tell it like it is.

In reviewing wildlife crime reportage covered in this book I have tried to use my experience with various aspects of policing to present a fair assessment of the cases covered and the outcomes of associated criminal investigations. This involves giving an accurate reflection on whether or not an incident is a crime, who might have reason to commit such an act, the incredible difficulties of gaining a conviction in some types of crime and whether certain wildlife crimes are in decline or becoming more common.

Though there is a wide range of crimes committed against wildlife I have concentrated on those associated with game management, particularly intensively managed grouse moors, and those with aspects of cruelty. These are some of the most difficult to detect and also the most difficult to prevent. As far as possible I have tried to keep the cases and incidents chronological within the thematic framework of the book but on occasions some overlap has been unavoidable.

As well as demonstrating where incorporating other agencies or experts into an investigation can be beneficial, I have also criticised what I suspect has been incompetent investigation. Though looking in from the sidelines now I have to try to balance what is presented in the media (which is not always accurate) with my investigative experience. I have also been complimentary to non-government organisations where they have been of valuable assistance in a police investigation. Conversely, I have been critical where I feel they have overstepped the mark.

For the record I am not against the shooting of game. I owned a .22 rifle until the late 1990s and a shotgun until 2014, though it was last used in 2011. As a teenager I used to help gamekeepers with their work. I enjoyed being outdoors and any work that involved animals, even though many of them – rabbits, foxes, stoats, weasels, grey squirrels, crows – ended up dead. I was also a keen beater, going regularly to grouse, pheasant and partridge shoots. I always had dogs, labradors and spaniels, and really enjoyed working them, either as a beater or behind the guns picking-up. Most of the keepers were decent, hard-working folks who, so far as I knew, stayed within the law. Since most knew I was a police officer it would have been pretty daft for them to have been openly involved in raptor persecution.

I often hear people criticising the fact that gamekeepers make no comment when interviewed by the police. As the law stands they are perfectly entitled to adopt this position, after all most hardened criminals have done this for years. Their defence team (regularly a specialist solicitor and sometimes a QC) may well be paid for by the landowner employing them or by a shooting or gamekeeping organisation but this is not a position unique to game management. I know the gamekeepers' main defence solicitors well. I have always found them to be perfectly reasonable and fair in their questioning in court, as are any of the QCs acting with them.

By the time I retired from Tayside Police in 2011 my opinion of driven grouse moors was at an all-time low. Despite having been a shooting person, seeing evidence of the amount of criminality associated with driven grouse shooting has turned me completely against that form of shooting. I knew the problematic driven grouse moors across Scotland but with my work between 2012 and 2015 on UK-wide crime intelligence while with NWCU I saw a much more comprehensive picture of wildlife crime on driven grouse moors in the north of England and the almost impossible task of getting those involved convicted. Dialogue with those involved in driven grouse management has had little success. Meantime the landowner, hiding behind his staff, is killing by proxy. One element of the crimes committed on shooting estates is clear: if estate owners *really* doesn't want their employees to kill birds of prey and sets out the consequences then it will not happen.

On driven grouse moors there is little evidence of change. While the licensing of shoots may help, the only real solution is the complete banning of driven grouse shooting.

By the end of this book I hope the reader will agree.

Alan Stewart
November 2017

PART 1

Cruelty, Blood Sports and Wildlife Crime

Cruelty to wild mammals is a major aspect of rural wildlife crime, crimes that include hare coursing, poaching, badger digging, illegal fox hunting, illegal snaring and illegal trapping. Very often the people involved in such offences are involved in other types of criminality, especially crimes of violence, drug dealing, dog fighting and cock fighting.

The motive of the criminals is principally 'sport', commonly referred to by the more accurate term of 'blood sport'. This is particularly the case in badger digging, fox hunting and hare coursing. Some hare coursing includes an element of gambling, though proof of this is hard to establish. There is considerable cruelty involved in snaring and trapping when it is carried out illegally. There is also a strong argument that legal snaring and trapping involves some cruelty, though, since the practice is legitimate, there is no remit for the police.

In some cases – hare coursing is a good example – such activities are embedded in the cultural tradition of the perpetrators, the 'sport' is being passed down from father to son (it's mostly boys that are inculcated, sometimes as young as aged seven or eight). This 'family tradition' is frequently used as an excuse in court, with one hare courser attempting to convince the court that it was legal so long as he only took one hare.

Deer and salmon poaching are usually based on profit, and the victims normally end up in the food chain with an associated health risk through lack of hygiene. The days of taking 'one for the pot' are long gone with most poachers exploiting deer and salmon as a relatively easy way of making money.

This type of crime is not normally associated with game management though occasionally the two overlap. With the exception of some of the illegal snaring or trapping crimes, these are situations where a gamekeeper, landowner or farmer is much more likely to be a valuable witness than a suspect. Ironically the most regular witness for the defence in hare coursing cases in Scotland is currently a retired gamekeeper.

Badger Digging

Incidents of badger digging regularly feature in the media, sometimes even in the form of boasts on social media from those involved in this sick activity. Badger digging involves horrendous cruelty. It is likely that some of the criminals involved will train their dogs in a similar way to which dogs used for fighting purposes are trained. This includes having them gripping and hanging from tyres to strengthen their neck muscles and running on a treadmill to build up their stamina. Most badger diggers, however, seem content to train their dogs to kill smaller and less powerful mammals such as cats and foxes, then graduate to badgers. They may even pit them against smaller dogs though this seems mostly to take place in the training of fighting dogs, with pet dogs sometimes being stolen for this purpose.

In Tayside some years ago the police dealt with a young gamekeeper who had made an artificial fox den on land beside his house. He had captured some fox cubs, took them home to the artificial den and had put his terrier into the den to kill them. He had also tied a ferret on to the end of a length of baler twine and set his terrier on it. Lastly, he had caught someone's cat and put it in a cage so that his terrier could tear at the cat through the cage. Worst of all, he had filmed all of these episodes for his continuing 'interest'. His fine of £200 in court was risible. Intelligence later indicated this man was involved in badger baiting so there was little doubt that this was what he was working up to.

Traditionally, there is comparatively little crime committed against badgers in Tayside though there have been a couple of setts dug out and another two instances of snares deliberately set for badgers. In these cases, had badgers been caught, their terrifying end would have been in the jaws of large dogs. There was also one complaint by a shooting tenant in Angus of gamekeepers from a nearby driven grouse moor on his land with guns, terriers and a spotlamp. He encountered them in their landrover hiding behind a wood. His opinion at the time was that they were after badgers but unfortunately he was unable to identify the men.

Combining England, Wales and Northern Ireland approximately 10% of the intelligence submitted to the National Wildlife Crime Unit (NWCU) relates to the persecution of badgers. In Scotland the figure is lower, probably nearer 5%. Not all of this is badger digging, but would include snaring, shooting, sett damage etc. The NWCU also shows that sometimes the same people are involved in dog fighting, but are more likely to be involved also in the taking of hares, rabbits and roe deer with their dogs. Many keep a range of dogs, from the smaller terriers that they use underground, often wearing locator collars, to much larger dogs to set on the luckless badger once it has been dug out from its sett, or simply to lamp and kill them when they are foraging at night. The dogs used are often bull lurchers, a cross between pitbull terrier-type dogs and lurchers. They are fast and strong and a badger would have little chance against even a single dog of this type.

A video was recovered from badger diggers in the north of England some years ago and the content was sickening. Thugs filmed themselves digging out two badgers from a sett. One was put in a pit dug out in the ground and stoned with large rocks until it was so badly injured it could barely fight back against the terrier that was then put in to torment it. The other was released and shot at with a shotgun, wounding it sufficiently that it had no chance against the pack of dogs set after it. The man with the shotgun was so reckless he was as likely to have shot his pal. Any decent person watching the video would be secretly wishing that he had!

Bull lurchers, lurchers and other large dogs involved in taking badgers invariably show some scarring, but the terriers, forced to fight underground, come off worst of all. They almost always show extreme facial scarring and loss of skin, muscle and even teeth. They seldom receive veterinary treatment since the vet would recognise the type of injuries and would be likely to contact the police. These people look upon a badly scarred dog as somewhat of a trophy. If their injuries are such that they can no longer fight or if they have shown any reluctance to do what is asked of them they would simply be killed by their owner.

Badger crime UK-wide is being fought through Operation Meles, an initiative involving the police, National Wildlife Crime Unit, the RSPCA, Badger Trust and other animal welfare groups. They are working together to gather evidence of baiting, which includes targeting 'hot spots', to track down offenders and prosecute them. They deserve every success, since the criminals involved are of the very worst type.

Proving a Badger Sett is 'In Current Use'

Many of the offences relating to any interference with a badger sett depend on the sett being proved as 'in current use' as opposed to being a sett that at some time in the distant or recent past held badgers.

To put in context the difficulties of proving that a badger sett is in current use, during March 2015 Lee Anthony Martin, described as a 'hunting devotee' in a report by ITV News, and the Gazette and Herald (a north of England newspaper), blocked entrance holes to a sett in woodland near Malton, North Yorkshire. The aim was to prevent a fox escaping from hounds and taking refuge there during the Middleton Hunt, due to take place on 29 March. Martin was arrested and charged with interfering with a badger sett.

Following a two-day trial at Scarborough Magistrates' Court in February 2016, Martin was found guilty, ordered to carry out 120 hours unpaid work and to pay £970 costs. His legal team appealed the conviction on the grounds there was no evidence that badgers were using the sett.

During the appeal hearing at York Crown Court, the judge heard evidence from independent experts on behalf of the pro-hunt Countryside Alliance and the League against Cruel Sports (LACS). Members of LACS had taken video footage showing signs of digging outside the sett which they said proved it was active. They also had night footage of a badger peering down one of the holes. The footage only showed that the sett was occupied up to 26 March and between 1 April and 5 April. Crucially, there was no evidence that the sett was in use on 29 March, the day it had been blocked.

The view of the appeal court was that, although it was obvious that Martin had blocked entrances to the sett, they did not think that the LACS evidence was sufficient to prove there were signs of current use by a badger. On this basis the appeal was granted and Martin's sentence revoked.

In this case then there were five days missing when it could not be proved that badgers were using the sett.

Badger setts can have one entrance or dozens. As an example, at one particular Perthshire badger sett, which is fairly typical of a very old and large sett, it is located in deciduous woodland and has over 20 entrances with literally tons of earth excavated, probably over many decades. A visitor to the sett can easily identify badger runs, latrines, claw marks and many more signs of badgers. There are several smaller outlying setts within about half a mile, all of which are used regularly by this family group, though in the case of the outlying setts they may not be used every day.

These signs can prove current use. This is the defined term in the Protection of Badgers Act necessary to establish a wildlife crime having been committed in relation to the sett. For investigative purposes the definition of a badger sett is the legislative definition: *any structure or place which displays signs indicating current use by a badger* (section 14). It is therefore the statutory requirement that for the structure or place to be a badger sett there must be *more than one sign or indicator* visibly present that point to the fact that the structure or place is being used by a badger (Sheriff's judgement, PF Jedburgh v Harris 2010). These signs could be:

- The presence of bedding
- Latrines or dung pits connected to the sett by recently-used paths
- Pad marks identifiable as those of a badger at the sett entrance
- Well-used paths with pad marks evidencing use by a badger
- Remnants of fresh bedding present in freshly excavated soil
- Hairs snagged in entrances or in freshly excavated soil
- Foraging marks
- The shape of the entrance
- A freshly-dug latrine pit even though there is no dung in it

The above list set out in the Jedburgh case is not exhaustive. If a piece of ground near a sett entrance was polished smooth by the badger sitting and having a good scratch there is no reason that this would not be acceptable in court as a further sign of current use, and may be one of several features of a sett in current use that has not been included in the list above. It is surprising that the shape of the entrance has been agreed by the sheriff as one of the relevant signs. The entrance shape may establish that the sett was dug by a badger but after that the shape is unlikely to vary much, even if deserted by badgers.

A sign near one sett that looked at first glance like a badger had been foraging was actually a scrape or 'couch' made by a roe deer before it sat down to rest. It would be important that an expert examining a sett that has been the subject of crime could differentiate between marks caused by badgers and by other mammals.

The decision by the appeal court seems very strange. The undisputed recent digging by a badger and the presence of a badger at the sett entrance should have been sufficient to prove current use. This is even more the case when using Natural England's guidelines. Though they are just guidelines and neither a sheriff's or magistrate's written judgement nor case law, they are eminently sensible. Natural England advice states:

It follows that 'current use' is not synonymous with 'current occupation'. To strictly equate the two would be nonsense, as a sett could alternate between being 'in use' during the day and 'not in use' at night (badgers forage each night and return to the sett each morning).

A further element to the definition of a sett in the Act is that it 'displays signs indicating' current use. In practical terms this will often be the key issue in deciding if a sett falls within the definition or not. A sett is defined as such (and thus protected) as long as signs indicative of 'current use' are present. Thus, a sett remains protected by the Act until such time as the signs (i.e. 'field signs') have deteriorated or decayed to such an extent that they no longer indicate that the sett is in 'current use'. Consequently, for a sett to fall within the definition in the Act, a badger need not be in current occupation, and may not have been for some time. As long as there are signs present indicating 'current use' the sett is defined as such in the Act and is therefore protected. The maximum lapse of time between last occupation by badgers and the inspection of a sett for it to be considered in 'current use' is how long it takes the signs to disappear, or more precisely, to appear so old as to not indicate 'current use.

In Scotland, Scottish Natural Heritage guidance states:

There is no case law to clarify what signs of current use means. For the purpose of this guidance, and in the absence of such case law, we consider that the presence of field signs such as bedding, fresh spoil heaps, signs of recent digging, hair, latrines, or footprints in or around the potential sett or evidence of badgers entering or exiting the structure or place in question would indicate current use of the structure / place by a badger.

In relation to the case, Countryside Alliance chief executive Tim Bonner is quoted as having said: 'This has been a huge waste of time and taxpayers' money'. Many will disagree with this statement, though there should be a learning experience here. Any police officer or other agency involved in the preparation of a badger-related case where proof of a badger sett is required should consider proof of current use as *absolutely crucial* to the case and obtain as much evidence as is possible to that end. The use of an ecologist well-experienced in badgers and their setts, engaged by the police to carry out a survey as soon as possible after the discovery that it had been blocked would probably have clinched this case.

Fox Hunting – a Sport Disguised as Pest Control

Early in 2014 the attempt to overturn or modify the Hunting Act 2004 in England and Wales began to gather pace. Scottish legislation preceded this Act by two years and only a handful of cases relating to foxes have come to court since that time. Evidence of wrongdoing is hard to establish and the complexity of the legislation certainly does not help. In fairness, the Protection of Wild Mammals (Scotland) Act 2002 has been used mostly in hare coursing cases but in 2011 the Nature Conservation (Scotland) Act amended the Wildlife and Countryside Act to create hare coursing and poaching offences that are more easily proved, at the same time putting the illegal taking of rabbits on a par with the illegal taking of hares.

It's widely accepted that mounted fox hunting is a sport rather than any serious attempt at fox control. The activity is controversial, with proponents seeing it as an important part of rural culture, and useful for reasons of conservation and pest control. Those who oppose mounted fox hunting argue that it is cruel and unnecessary. There are much more effective means of controlling foxes through snaring, (even though this method offends many people) dealing with cubs and often the vixen and/or dog fox at a den, or lamping foxes at night. Lamping is probably the most effective and humane method of fox control but of course there are areas where this cannot be undertaken because of the terrain. In Scotland and in the north of England, 'foot packs' of hounds are regularly used to control foxes. This is the use of a pack of hounds controlled by me or women on foot to flush foxes forward towards a considerable number of strategically placed guns. This has always been done purely for fox control and seldom appears to deviate from the law.

A study relating to fox control by Dr David Macdonald of Bristol University, *Running with the Fox* (1987), one of many on the subject of vulpine ecology, shows that social factors in a fox group are probably the main influence on fox numbers, with only the dominant pair being the most likely to breed. The same conclusion is reached in a later study by the International Fund for Animal Welfare (IFAW), working with Bristol and York Universities. Backing this up to a degree, though unintentionally, are reports from gamekeepers who state they shoot or snare a particular number of foxes every year on the estate where they work. One gamekeeper shot 40 a year on the hill land for which he had working responsibility. If this is fox *control* why was the number not lessening every year as one would expect? The answer of course is that he was generating a vacuum which was filled probably as quickly as he was creating the vacancies. It was puzzling why he bothered at all as the estate reared very few pheasants. Extra time on good husbandry might have been better use of the time, and in any case there was a huge rabbit population on the hill which would be by far the main food supply of the foxes. Unquestionably, some sheep and poultry keepers can have bother with foxes but again good husbandry – simple things like ensuring poultry flocks are inside at night and bringing lambs inside during their first week or so of their life – can limit predation.

This strongly suggests that the claim that fox hunting on horseback, with the participants dressed in their finery, is done for the purpose of fox control is a sham. It is done for no reason other than sport, albeit a cruel one, and a 'good day out'.

Relaxing the Law: England and Wales

One of the proposed relaxations in the current 2004 Act in England and Wales is to allow a fox to be flushed from cover by more than two dogs. This is currently the position in Scotland provided the dogs are under control. This means that if the dogs chase the fox in any direction other than towards waiting guns they should be stopped and recalled, otherwise an offence is committed. Whether that offence can be proved is another matter. It is rather odd that there is this difference between the two pieces of legislation. There seem to be fewer complaints of illegal fox hunting in Scotland and as will be seen later a report commissioned to look at the difficulties in policing fox hunting in Scotland made no adverse comment about the number of hounds involved. Whether there are two or twenty hounds involved it is their manner of use that results in illegality.

One of the most obscene parts of this charade relates to the digging out of a fox that has gone to ground to escape the hounds. If a fox has escaped in this manner – and bear in mind this is a sport, not pest control – it should be left and an acknowledgment made that the animal has bettered the hounds. The fact that on some occasions the fox is dug out and thrown live to the hounds makes digging out the fox even more abhorrent. There is a difference between this and fox control at dens in spring time, where the vixen may be shot and the cubs killed by a single terrier since this is considered in law to be a genuine form of pest control. There are normally only two or three people involved, no horses or cacophonous horns and no entourage of spectators out for a day's entertainment.

Stag hunting with hounds seems most predominant in the south-west of England. This is even more Victorian than fox hunting and it is astonishing that the practice is permitted to continue. Red deer are hardly pests, and because of the increased adrenaline after a chase the beast may not even be worth eating.

Scotland in well ahead with improvements in wildlife legislation, with more recent amendments tending to reduce suffering on wild animals and at the same time making the law more enforceable. With a Conservative government in Westminster, champions of the hunting and shooting fraternity, England and Wales are more likely to see the scrapping of hunting legislation rather than tightening it up.

Foxhunting in Scotland

At the end of May 2015, a number of foxhunts in Scotland had been monitored by the League against Cruel Sports (LACS), who claim that in many cases the law was being ignored.

The legislation allows a fox to be flushed from cover above ground by a dog or dogs *under control* and driven towards guns to be shot. Those participating must *act to ensure that the fox is shot* but an offence is not created if the fox is shot at and missed, or if it changes direction away from the waiting guns. If, in the process of chasing the fox towards the guns, the hounds catch and kill the fox, no offence is committed. These exceptions make building a prosecution case exceptionally difficult and frustrate people who have witnessed what they are convinced is illegal hunting.

A case seems clear-cut if no guns are in place but the wording *dog under control* should be borne in mind. The term 'under control' is interesting. In terms of Section 10(4) of the Act (definitions) a dog is under control if the person responsible for the dog is able to direct the dog's activity by physical contact or verbal or audible command, or if the dog is carrying out a series of actions appropriate to the activity undertaken, having been trained to do so.

In one case LACS considered that a clear offence by a particular hunt had been taking place and rightly passed the evidence to the police for further investigation. Police officers have to uphold the law as it stands, not as some might like it to be. They must be completely impartial, separating legal issues from moral concerns. These investigations can be further complicated by the number of potential suspects involved and, in real time incidents, the fact that where the alleged offence is occurring may not be easily accessible and the speed at which the activity may be moving forward.

In an article in the *Sunday Herald* of 15 October 2017 the League against Cruel Sports claim that their observation of fox hunting in 2016/17 discovered two new methods to assist in breaking – or at least bending – the law to enable a fox to be pursued and killed by hounds. Firstly they claim that they have observed members of the hunt who:

> rode around on quad bikes firing shots in the air to give the impression the hunt was shooting at foxes while hounds pursued them.

Secondly they report a 'new development' where hunts claimed foxes were wounded by gunshot before dogs tore them apart. The article goes on to state that:

> there is a provision in the Protection of Wild Mammals (Scotland) Act 2002 which allows packs of hounds to kill a wounded animal.

This, in fact, is arguable and confirms the point made by Lord Bonomy that there is abuse and exploitation of the current law.

There are many drawbacks with the 2002 legislation. It was a private members bill prepared and completed in a hurry and with insufficient consultation. The Act is basically a list of three offences with pages of exemptions and exceptions. With so few cases having been to court the legislation remains largely untested.

Captive Fox Cubs

In June 2015 the League against Cruel Sports reported to the police that 16 fox cubs were being held in a barn near Malton in North Yorkshire. They claimed that the shed was fitted out to resemble a fox den, with large pipes and other items in which the cubs could hide. They also claimed that the cubs were being fed by the terrier man for the Middleton Foxhounds. The land on which the shed is located is owned by Lord Middleton, with the shed being 200 yards away from the hunt kennels.

So why would anyone want to keep 16 fox cubs, which are probably from three litters? Provided they are well looked after there is nothing illegal in doing so. In an article in the *Daily Mirror*, Lord Middleton, when asked if the foxes were being kept so they could later be hunted, said, 'That's rubbish. We're not allowed to hunt foxes with hounds. They're not being kept for hunting. It's not illegal to keep foxes'. He said that he 'had no idea whatsoever' the cubs were being kept on his land, but added that they were not being mistreated. He did not 'condone' keeping foxes, and suggested the cubs were being cared for by the Hunt for kind reasons. 'I think people have rung up and said, 'Hey, look I've got foxes that need rescuing, their mother's dead', or, 'I can't live with them where they are, can you look after them?' The Hunt obviously has a supply of meat from farmers etc and it would be able to feed and look after them and then release them back to the wild.'

A respectable lord of the manor wouldn't tell lies or mislead the public, would he? He certainly wouldn't break the law by rearing fox cubs to release for hounds to chase and kill. Would he?

The cubs were seized by the police while they investigated the matter. The intended fate of the cubs was completely different to that which Lord Middleton claimed. Not even the most trusting person would believe what he is alleged to have said, and in fact it is an insult to their intelligence. What is unfortunate is that at the conclusion of the police investigation there is very unlikely to be evidence of an offence since, as explained above, there is no offence in taking or keeping fox cubs. Had there been evidence they were being cruelly treated the outcome could have been different. On this occasion the cubs were saved from certain death by hounds or terriers but on how many other occasions has this reprehensible and uncivilised behaviour taken place?

A similar disgraceful scenario occurred the following June, this time involving the South Herefordshire Hunt. The Hunt Investigation Team (HIT), described as 'a small, specialist, highly trained team committed to exposing the truth about fox hunting and other cruel bloodsports' had filmed hunt staff bringing wild foxes to the hunt kennels. They had also filmed a young fox in a cage and were of the view initially that the hunt was repopulating the area with foxes, which, if common practice as claimed by HIT, casts even more distrust on the claim of fox hunting being carried out for fox control.

The team continued to carry out surveillance on the kennels and within a short time they saw that the hunt had four captive foxes. Disturbing footage was then recorded of foxes being removed from the cage with a grasper and being moved around the site, at which point HIT made contact with the police and RSPCA. After discussion, the police decided there was insufficient evidence of an offence but asked the Hunt Investigation Team to continue monitoring the situation

Footage obtained a few days later suggested that two cubs aged between six and ten weeks had been taken into the hound block where it was believed they had been thrown alive to the hounds. Footage also showed hunt personnel throwing the dead bodies of the foxes into a commercial waste bin on the site, next to the kennel block.

In the early hours of that morning the team spoke with the police and RSPCA and it was decided that there was now enough evidence to act. To ensure evidence was not lost the HIT team returned to the site and retrieved the bodies of the cubs from the waste bin. The dead foxes were handed to the police as their mangled bodies and the subsequent post mortem results would form a crucial part of the evidence.

The police and RSPCA raided the hunt kennels in the days following. In total five arrests were made, evidence seized and a case was submitted by Hereford CID. In November 2017 the case is still pending.

The Law on Fox Hunting is 'in Tatters'

2015 was an eventful year for the debate on fox hunting, and at the end of that year a BBC news article reported a claim by the Countryside Alliance (CA) that support for fox hunting was a strong as ever. Apparently, more than 90% of the 300 hunts surveyed claimed they hunted at least the same number of days as before the ban on hunting. The allegation by the CA is that the hunting law is 'in tatters'.

In the article the CA's chief executive is quoted as saying, '(The Act) was never about foxes or animal welfare but rather as an attempt to eradicate hunts and the communities that surround them.' Whilst this view is understandable in the circumstances, there is no question that in introducing the ban animal welfare was paramount.

Further proof of the devious and illegal methods of fox hunting was the discovery by the League against Cruel Sports (LACS) in the middle of December 2015 of a fox held captive in an unused brick building on the Buckminster Estate near to where the Belvoir Hunt meet. LACS informed the police and monitored the building. On

16 December, the day before the hunt was due to meet, a man was seen coming to the building to check on the fox. LACS then removed the fox and watched on the day of the hunt. They saw the same man return with a sack and a pole with a net attached...

So, if the Acts (if we include the Hunting Act 2004 in England and Wales and the Protection of Wild Mammals (Scotland) Act 2002) are indeed in tatters, they need urgent repair. For a start why not limit the hunting of foxes with dogs to people on foot? There's no need for horses and a fancy dress parade. If that doesn't work, and drag hunting is used as a cover to hunt foxes, then there may be ways of guaranteeing that activity stays within the law by ensuring there are independent observers. This may be achievable in Scotland, which is beset by fewer problems. It may be too much to ask of a government in England and Wales.

Foxhunting Incident in the Scottish Borders

A report in March 2016 by BBC Scotland featuring alleged criminal activity by a mounted fox hunt in the Scottish Border must have appalled all who watched it. On two occasions a pack of hounds apparently chasing a fox was filmed by the League against Cruel Sports. Shocking though this was, it has been long suspected that this and other breaches of the law are carried out regularly by some – or many – mounted hunts. In this case two men were charged under the Protection of Wild Mammals (Scotland) Act 2002 by officers of Police Scotland.

Father and son John Richardson, who is 67 and whipper-in of the Jedforest Hunt, and Johnathan Riley, who is 24 and huntsman in charge of the Jedforest Hunt, were those charged in connection with the Scottish Borders incident and appeared at Jedburgh Sheriff Court in October 2016. They pleaded not guilty. Filmed footage and detailed comment regarding the incident was all over the media; even more so on social media. Courts tend not to like this comprehensive publicity in advance of a trial and there will be certain aspects of it that will be strong ammunition for defence solicitors. Similarly, the use of video footage taken on private land may well prove to be an obstacle to conviction.

The trial started at Selkirk Sheriff court on 16 March 2017, with Sheriff Peter Paterson on the bench. Witness Peter Cross had filmed the incident on a video camera from a covert situation at a distance of 650 metres. Since there is a need for corroboration he was accompanied by witness Terry Hill. They filmed footage of a fox being chased into an earth (a fox den) by the hounds and then a man spending around 40 minutes digging to locate the fox. This is permitted but when the fox is found it must be dispatched humanely and not released for hounds to chase.

In spite of the terms of the legislation the footage showed the fox being released from the hole and pursued by the hounds. The fox went out of sight behind a ridge – a blind spot for the cameramen – and its fate could not be confirmed.

PC Jamie Hood, who at that time was wildlife crime officer for the Borders area, told the court, 'A fox can be flushed by dogs from cover to guns. My opinion from the footage… is that the fox is pursued by a number of hounds across open ground with one or two horsemen and other persons present. The pursuit is beyond what is allowed in the exception.' He stated that he could not hear any gunshots on the videos during the incidents or see any sign of gunmen.

PC Hood returned to the area three weeks later and discovered the carcass of a fox in the dead ground area where the fox had last been seen. Three weeks is a long time for a follow-up search and all that was remaining was part of the vertebrae and three legs with red fur round the paws. He said a post-mortem examination was carried out on the carcass and there was no evidence that the fox had been shot. An x-ray or post-mortem examination on the complete body of a fox would have been much more conclusive. He agreed under cross-examination from the defence that he could not say for certain that it was the same fox which the video had shown being pursued by the dogs.

A former retired wildlife crime officer, Malcolm Henderson, told the court he had been at the hunt with a shotgun as one of the guns required under the legislation. He said he had been standing in the dip where the fox disappeared.

Mr Richardson, one of the accused, told the court that there was a gunman, Mr Henderson, in the dip who shot at and wounded the fox before it was accounted for by the hounds. Richardson claimed that the hounds had been used to flush out the foxes and 'evict them towards the gun'.

After a total of eight days of evidence the trial concluded on 29 June, 2017. Because of the use of covert video footage a guilty verdict was still in doubt. It was a pleasant surprise when both men were found guilty of a charge relating to two incidents of hunting a wild mammal with a dog or dogs, with Riley being fined £400 and Richardson being fined £250.

The sheriff made his ruling on the evidence of two incidents in the video footage, the first being when the fox was chased by the hounds and took refuge in an earth. Riley had claimed in his evidence that he could recall the hounds whenever it was necessary as he had them under control. It is an essential element in the legislation that when hunting the hounds must be 'under control.' The sheriff stated: 'He (Riley) allowed the hounds to take up the chase and deliberately chose not to recall them. That being the case, in my opinion the charge is proven beyond reasonable doubt.'

In the second incident, when the fox was dug out from the earth, Sheriff Paterson said there was another breach of the legislation. 'The fox's hole is visible to the huntsman. When the fox emerges, the hounds are intentionally released by the huntsman. The fox is visible to the huntsman after it was released and, in my opinion, was not in cover when it emerged from the hole. Accordingly, in my opinion, this constitutes a breach of the act.'

The sheriff was also critical of the gunman's position, saying he did not accept that the fox was shot as soon as possible. He concluded: 'In my opinion, this second incident amounted to a deliberate act to allow hounds to pursue the fox in breach of the legislation. In submissions, I heard no argument which could justify the immediate and deliberate release of the hounds when the fox emerged, other than it was immediately in cover, which, in my opinion, it was manifestly not.'

It is likely that the sheriff meant that the person with the gun should have been much closer to the hole to shoot the fox as soon as it emerged. To accomplish this safely hounds, horses and spectators would have to be cleared from the area to allow a shot at the fox without endangering any person or other animal. Taking the hounds off to a safe distance would mean that they would be unable to pursue the fox when it was dug out and bolted. This was not done and allowed the offence to take place when otherwise the fox could have been shot.

This conviction was the first in Scotland in relation to offences committed by an organised fox hunt since the legislation came into force in 2002. That it has taken 15 years before a conviction demonstrates the complicated nature of the legislation and the urgent need for it to be made far more suited to dealing with its alleged breaches.

Both men indicated that they would appeal. Could the appeal have been on the grounds of the use of the covert filming on private land without permission and other than by an investigative agency under the terms of RIP(S)A? If so a decision by an appeal court, if the appeal fails, may have benefits for the detection of other wildlife crime by the use of covert surveillance, particularly raptor persecution. We will never know, as the appeal was withdrawn at the beginning of October 2017.

Fox Hunting Proposals in Scotland

In November 2016, Lord Bonomy's report, commissioned by the Scottish Government to look at the wording of the Protection of Wild Mammals (Scotland) Act 2002 and the difficulties for enforcement, was completed. The aim of the legislation in 2002 was to bring to an end the chasing and killing of wild mammals by dogs, and was primarily aimed at mounted fox hunting.

As the Tayside Police wildlife crime officer, the author was asked by Scottish Government just days before the 2002 bill became law to comment on it. At first glance, with only three offences within the proposed legislation, enforcement looked straightforward. However, the offences were followed by numerous and complex exceptions, which very quickly made it clear that enforcement in relation to fox hunting would be anything but simple.

For dealing with the crime of hare coursing there were many improvements over the poaching legislation, particularly with the introduction of a power of arrest and far stronger penalties. Police officers had plenty of experience of the excuse that hare coursers would offer since rabbits were not included as mammals in the bill, especially when someone was searching for hares to course: 'We're no looking for hares, we're looking for rabbits.' That was trotted out with monotonous regularity. In an upgraded version, in the middle of the night in Perthshire the police caught some Glasgow criminals with their dogs. They had a dead hare in the footwell of the car and exclaimed mock surprise, saying they thought they had caught a particularly big rabbit.

Two of the recommendations the author made in 2002 were to augment the term 'deliberate' with the term 'reckless', bringing the legislation into line with other wildlife laws, and not to exclude the rabbit as a mammal, but to create a general licence for the taking of rabbits by dogs provided the person doing so was authorised. Neither of these suggestions was taken up. It was probably too late for any alterations by that time anyway, so we were left with legislation that, at least as far as mounted foxhunting was concerned, was almost unworkable.

Lord Bonomy was scrupulously fair in his report. It was heartening that he agreed that the term 'deliberately' needs to be augmented by 'reckless' or some similar interpretation. The suggested restriction in the report to the use of only one dog underground made sense by way of ensuring fox control is more humane, and increasing the time bar to three years in line with the Wildlife and Countryside Act would allow investigations to still get to court where there were unavoidable delays due to post-mortem examinations and the preparation of specialist reports.

Other welcome suggestions in the report are that an accused person should have to prove that claims of illegal conduct fall within one of the exceptions, and that the owner of land where an offence takes place may be vicariously liable. Arguably the most effective change would be the implementation of the proposal for official hunt monitors to be employed.

In addition to any changes to the 2002 Act there is a strong likelihood, because of the recent Penalties Review, that considerably increased penalties will shortly be available to the courts to deal with anyone who thinks the law can be ignored.

On 31 January 2017 Cabinet Secretary for Environment, Climate Change and Land Reform Roseanna Cunningham announced that the operation and enforcement of the Protection of Wild Mammals (Scotland) Act 2002 is to be strengthened. In a press release Ms Cunningham said:

> I am determined to ensure the highest possible levels of animal welfare and Lord Bonomy's recommendations will help us build on the advances already achieved.

This package of measures will substantially improve the language used in the existing legislation, address inconsistencies in the law, and strengthen the scrutiny and accountability of hunts.

A code of conduct will be developed and the possibilities of a new monitoring scheme will be explored. As of October 2017, Ministers have now opened a public consutation on the proposed changes to the existing legislation, which include:

- The introduction of vicarious liability and reverse burden of proof provisions
- An extension to the time limit for bringing prosecutions The removal of inconsistencies and the improvement of definitions

The Scottish Government and Scottish Parliament are again leading the way on wildlife legislation within the UK.

Snares

The legislation governing the use of snares is the Wildlife and Countryside Act 1981. Despite the legislation there has been astonishing unprofessionalism by some snare users, the principal offences over the years being failure to check the snares within the required maximum intervals. This has led to horrendous suffering by victims, which were often left in unchecked snares for days or even longer. In one of the worst examples attended by the author, in 2003 a gamekeeper set fox snares on a hillside fence bordering a wood in springtime. In the autumn a walker found a desiccated fox and badger in the snares and reported the matter. When the suspect was interviewed by the police he admitted setting the snares but said that he hadn't managed to get time to go back and check them, this despite the passage of at least five months.

In Scotland, under the Nature Conservation (Scotland) Act 2004, changes were made to improve snaring legislation and began to make some difference. These changes particularly addressed the issue of self-locking snares, ensured a victim was removed from the snare at each check and introduced the offence of knowingly causing or permitting an offence.

In 2011, under the Wildlife and Natural Environment (Scotland) Act 2011, many more improvements were made to snaring legislation, this time ensuring that all operators had been trained, that they had registered with the police, that they attached their registration number to each snare and that they kept records of where each snare was set and of any victim caught. This series of changes has undoubtedly led to increased professionalism, with a smaller number of complaints made to the police. It is disgraceful that equivalent legislation in England and Wales has fallen well behind that in Scotland.

There have always been non-target animals caught unintentionally (though sometimes carelessly). This can be reduced considerably through the use of snares adapted to break away if a mammal heavier than a fox – for instance a badger – is caught. The manner in which the snare breaks ensures that the creature is released without retaining any part of the snare, which is extremely important. The use, at least as yet, of break-away snares is not mandatory.

The Glenogil Estate Snaring Case

Glenogil Estate, an intensively managed driven grouse moor, has been at the centre of many investigations into wildlife crime. One of the most recent was a case relating to the snaring of a deer (dead in the snare) and two foxes, one dead and one still alive, found in September 2014. The case was submitted by the SSPCA and was dropped by the Crown in March 2016. The basis of the case submitted was that William Curr, the Glenogil gamekeeper allegedly responsible for the snares, had failed to inspect the snare which had killed a deer, had failed to keep a record of finding a deer in a snare and had failed to check another snare for more than 24 hours, during which time a fox became trapped and died of dehydration.

Using investigative experience and details from *The Courier*, the newspaper covering Tayside and Fife, and from the animal welfare charity OneKind, the chronology of the investigation is likely to have been as follows:

The field officer for the charity OneKind was alerted to a dead deer which had allegedly been found in a snare. An offence may not have been committed at this point as deer are sometimes caught in snares by accident.

He had visited the estate 'to look for legal snares as part of the OneKind campaign to expose their cruelty'.

He appears to have found the dead deer in the snare, a line of set fox snares, a dead fox in a snare and a fox, still live, in another one. The live fox had been caught round the abdomen and the snare had cut in to the flesh. It appears these incidents were corroborated as a report states that 'the witnesses called the SSPCA.' Since there was a live or injured animal involved he was justified in doing so rather than – or in addition to – calling the police though it is still not clear from this further information whether or not an offence had been committed.

Someone from the SSPCA attended and humanely despatched the injured fox

It is likely that the three carcasses were seized by the SSPCA so that it could be established whether or not they had been in the snares for more than the permitted period of 24 hours (snares must be checked at least once at intervals of not more than 24 hours and anything caught must be removed). It appears the fox found dead had died from dehydration, unlikely to have occurred within 24 hours.

The tag details on the snares would be noted (this gives a number registered by the police as the user and indicates for which species the snare is set). There is a presumption that the user of a snare is the person obtaining the tag number from the police.

The snares may have been submitted for DNA examination, though unless already on record, to obtain a DNA sample from the suspect for comparison, he would need to have been detained or arrested by the police.

A request would be made to Police Scotland for the snare tag details, including records of which species had previously been caught and where they were caught. A person using snares must produce these records to a police officer, if requested, within 21 days.

The suspect, Curr, would be interviewed regarding the incidents, though is not required to comment.

A report is then submitted to the procurator fiscal.

The case was due for trial on 9 May 2016, but on 10 March the Crown Office indicated it was not going to proceed with the case.

Assuming, evidentially, all the points have been covered, the stumbling block is most likely to have been procedure. There have been wildlife cases in the past where the Crown Office or court has not accepted the evidence of a member of the public going on to land *to look for* offences, which is different to a person being on land for the purpose of a leisure or study activity and coming across such evidence.

In this case the procedure would have been much more failsafe if the OneKind field officer had informed the police of the likelihood of a dead deer in a snare and had accompanied a police officer to the scene (as indeed the author has done successfully along with a divisional wildlife crime officer and the OneKind field officer). In the circumstances this could have been carried out without application for a search warrant.

There is also the issue of a sheriff's written judgement in 2007 (PF Peebles v Andrew Crawford Struthers). In this case the court held that entry by SSPCA without warrant to alleviate the suffering of an animal is perfectly proper. However, if during that process it appears that evidence should be gathered for a prosecution a warrant should be sought before that is done. In the Struthers case the SSPCA had gone to a farm after finding some dead sheep in a field. They took various photographs, called on the assistance of another inspector and plotted the position of the carcasses on a rough plan. In all they took 66 photographs and seized three carcasses for post mortem examination. The sheriff's view was that the evidence was obtained illegally. There was no urgency, since they could have left someone watching over the evidence and obtained a warrant.

There may be similarities in the Glenogil investigation, though the court may have taken a different view to the Struthers case since it appears that while SSPCA and OneKind were dealing with the incident, gamekeepers from the estate had arrived and a confrontation took place, with the head gamekeeper implying that the OneKind field officer and the local contacts must have set the snares themselves. In these circumstances it could be argued that there were not enough SSPCA and OneKind staff to both guard the evidence and apply for a warrant.

The investigation of this incident may have been a 'test run' in the hope of demonstrating that SSPCA can adequately deal with wildlife crime. The lesson to be learned for future similar incidents in which OneKind is involved, especially if they occur on driven grouse moors, is to ensure that a police officer is involved from the outset.

Alleged Theft of a Fox Snare

In a September 2016 copy of the *Sunday Post* there was a report of a 63-year-old woman being charged by police after releasing a fox from a snare. The circumstances reported were that earlier in the year she was walking in the Pentland Hills in West Lothian when she found the fox caught by the waist in a snare. She felt sorry for the fox and is quoted as saying, 'I had presumed these barbaric things were illegal and did what most people would have done. I called the Scottish SPCA and they asked me to give the snare to them.'

It seems that SSPCA then investigated the legality of the snare's use.

The police learned of the incident, though it is not clear from the news report when this was, or indeed if they were aware that another organisation was already involved in the investigation.

Police officers called on the woman, allegedly at 10.30 pm, and charged her with theft of the snare.

From the details of the news report there is nothing to suggest that the snare was other than set legally, even though the victim was caught round the middle. The report states that '[the law] limits where [snares] can be placed and how animals are caught, with many experts interpreting the law to rule out foxes being trapped round the abdomen'. A snare can be set perfectly legally and professionally and still catch a fox other than round the neck. Ultimately the decision to prosecute or to convict would be up to the prosecutor and/or a court.

Neither the police nor SSPCA considered a report to the procurator fiscal for the illegal setting of the snare, though the police clearly considered the offence of theft of the snare had taken place.

To prove a theft, there needs to be *mens rea*. The legal definition of *mens rea* is *'an element of criminal responsibility, a guilty mind; a guilty or wrongful purpose; a criminal intent: guilty knowledge or wilfulness.'* In other words a suspect needs to be aware that his or her conduct is criminal. It's doubtful that this could be established in this incident. The inclination of nearly everyone who walks in the country and finds an animal trapped would be to release it. There may be nothing illegal about the capture of the animal but human nature, in most cases, would be to feel pity for it and to try to relieve its suffering. (It's worth remarking that the woman did well, working on her own, to release what was no doubt a struggling fox from a snare, and presumably without being bitten.) This is probably what was going through the woman's mind, plus it is hardly likely that a person who is aware of her guilt would hand over the evidence most likely to prove that guilt.

This appears to be a badly flawed judgement by the police officer to charge the woman. It is also a completely unreasonable time of night to call on anyone, with a few exceptions such as by prior arrangement, to deliver an urgent message or if the person has committed a serious offence. Most folks are in bed by this hour and would be most alarmed – or at the very least annoyed – by a knock on the door. The police reaction seems to have been completely out of proportion to the incident. Thankfully the charge was withdrawn, though not before the woman had an extensive period of worry.

The SSPCA: Additional Powers or Not?

In the four or so years up to 2017 SSPCA have been trying to increase their powers. Their powers allow them, without warrant, to enter land to relieve the suffering of an animal. Examples would be farm animals in a field with insufficient food, a badger being baited by dogs, a live fox caught in an illegal snare or corvids caught and held in a cage trap beyond 24 hours or without sufficient food, water or shelter. Scottish Government has been asked to increase SSPCA powers without warrant. If the increase in powers is granted this would allow them to enter land to investigate a report that relates to animals already dead and is clearly going beyond animal welfare. This would include a dead animal in a snare or trap. Their powers without warrant in this respect would be broadly similar to that of the police.

There are strong views for and against this proposal. Firstly the SSPCA is a charity and are much less accountable than the police. Should non-government organisations (NGOs) really be involved in a search of someone's property? In its day, Tayside Police used the services of RSPB and SSPCA to assist with searches. As far as was possible they did not come into contact with suspects and were mainly utilised for field searches or for the examination of dogs or other animals. If they were used in the search of a house, it was under the direction of a police officer and for some specific item or items where their knowledge was likely to surpass that of the police officers.

Police officers can take any other people they require with them on a search. If SSPCA had increased powers would this include an identical power to take others with them? A situation could arise where a search of farm buildings or a series of sheds and outhouses could be conducted by SSPCA together with, say, staff of RSPB, Scottish Badgers, LACS etc, all charities and with no police officer present. Would that really be acceptable?

Incidentally, there have been cases where SSPCA special investigations staff, when they want to carry out a search where only the police have the statutory power, have circumvented specialist wildlife crime officers to request assistance from a constable at the police station nearest to the incident. In these cases, though the police officer is the holder of the powers of search, he or she is likely to have little or no specialist knowledge of wildlife crime and is basically led by SSPCA. This is completely wrong, and if the search goes badly then the officer, who has the powers and should be directing the search, would be left as the person responsible.

Importantly, as appears in the release of the fox and alleged theft of the snare just discussed, it is highly likely that two organisations, at least for some of the time, were involved each without the knowledge of the other organisation. This happened to be a very low-level incident but many wildlife criminals are involved in serious and organised crime and in some cases police spend months building sufficient intelligence, then evidence, to gain a conviction. Disruption of a planned or intended police operation by another agency, albeit with the best of intentions, could put months or even years of work at risk.

On 1 March 2017 the Green Party MSP Andy Wightman tabled a parliamentary motion that the Scottish Government grant further powers to the SSPCA. This was reported on the blog Raptor Persecution UK and there were some curious comments on the blog following the announcement. The blog has many excellent contributors but, like comments on most blogs and media articles, there are always some that the writers should just retain as thoughts and not commit to print, for example:

They (SSPCA) need powers to enter land without permission to do spot checks. *So* many bird traps, spring traps, rabbit drop traps and snares are set illegally that it might make estate owners pause for thought – what with the risk of vicarious liability.

Even the police have no powers 'to enter land without permission to do spot checks; they must have reasonable suspicion. It's hardly likely that such powers would be granted to a charity. Further, snares and traps for mammals are not offences for which vicarious liability can be considered.

The SSPCA already have a Special Investigations Unit with experience in following up wildlife crimes, it includes a couple of ex policemen who would ensure there were no evidential/procedural problems with working under increased powers. These are the people who would investigate raptor killing, not the ordinary inspectorate...

The point about experienced staff is true, but SSPCA do not have access to the required level of staffing, or to the forensic assistance that's available to the police. Let's say the SSPCA were granted the powers they request. They then undertake an investigation into a poisoned eagle on a driven grouse moor with seven gamekeepers, two shepherds and two tenant farmers any of whom could be a suspect. If there is reasonable cause to narrow suspicion to, say four, of these folks how would the five or so SSPCA special investigations staff manage to co-ordinate simultaneous searches of them, their buildings, their vehicles, take sweepings from vehicles and vacuuming of clothing for traces of pesticide, carry out possible search of 30,000 acres of moorland, take fingerprints or DNA samples that might be required (which they have no power to do and which requires a suspect to have been detained or arrested by the police). In parallel would they consider vicarious liability and search for documents likely to prove this offence, then in due course undertake the complex investigation required to convict a landowner or sporting agent. Is this one they would bat back to the police as too difficult? If SSPCA got more powers would they be able to pick and choose the incidents they will attend?

To suggest that SSPCA can replicate what police officers do is simplistic. This is not a straightforward issue and it is not that SSPCA inspectors (across the board rather than just the special investigations staff) should not get *any* new powers, but if granted these should be targeted to allow them, if they are already on an animal welfare investigation and find evidence of a wildlife crime, to extend their search to gather evidence which they can then hand over to the police. That would fulfil their role as an animal welfare charity as well as being of considerable assistance in another aspect of crime investigation.

In May 2017, after lengthy consideration by Scottish Government, the request for extra powers for SSPCA officers was refused.

Hare Coursing

In October 2016, *The Courier* carried the story of an appeal by a convicted man against the severity of his sentence for hare coursing, which took place in Perthshire. Mark Reid had been jailed for four months and banned from keeping dogs for six years after a court heard during trial how he and his son, plus two others who were cleared after the trial, had been coursing in a field west of Perth. The son, John Stewart, was banned from keeping dogs for two years and ordered to carry out 100 hours' unpaid work.

Reid admitted three previous convictions for wildlife crime, and his solicitor told the court, 'He has a previous conviction for this activity from Forfar (Sheriff Court) and he comes from a background where this activity has, to an extent, been normalised.'

How many times have such pleas in mitigation been made in court by defence solicitors, and how many times have officers involved in the cases thought, 'Have you ever heard such bloody guff!' Most sheriffs or magistrates probably say the same thing under their breath.

At his appeal, Reid's solicitor said that the jail term was excessive and that the convicted man had managed to pay fines in the past. A fine, of course, is usually much preferred by a convicted person to a jail term. The solicitor also told the court that Reid was not fit to perform unpaid work as he has trouble with his back. She omitted to say that his bad back doesn't affect his hare coursing, which must include climbing fences. Neither does it affect his ability to obtain money for fines.

The appeal court accepted that Reid should not have been jailed, quashed his conviction and instead imposed a fine of £1500. His six-year ban on keeping dogs still stands. This is really in Reid's own interests as dogs could easily pull on the lead and make his bad back worse.

Fines do not seem to bother hare coursers. They are normally paid up at £5 or £10 a week and this makes their criminal activity, already low risk from being caught, also low risk of meaningful punishment. Frequently four or five people are involved in hare coursing. Even if all are caught the two with least number of analogous convictions plead guilty. This reduces the level of fine, which is probably split in any case amongst all those involved.

Imprisonment is inconvenient for most criminals. It is also unusual as a sentence in hare coursing since courts are encouraged not to send people to jail for short sentences and to utilise non-custodial methods of punishment. By far the most effective method of punishment is to ban the individual from keeping dogs. Owning a fast dog for coursing seems to elevate the standing of these individuals with their peers and they try every trick in the book to avoid their dogs getting seized.

The next most effective punishment is to disqualify the individual from driving. Courts have this power if the person is using a vehicle for the purposes of committing crime. One courser, in addition to a fine, was disqualified from driving for two years. He was heartily sick and appealed the severity of the sentence. The appeal court reduced the disqualification to one year, still an effective sentence.

Lastly the vehicle being used can be seized by the police at the time and subsequently forfeited by the court. This can be effective if the car has some value, though most of the vehicles used are worth only a few hundred pounds since the coursers (and many other types of criminals as well) are aware of this potential penalty.

OneKind: How to Stop Hare Coursing

OneKind's website states that: 'OneKind is Scotland's leading animal campaigns charity. We are based in Edinburgh, with volunteers across Scotland and the UK, and our work covers Scotland's wildlife, farm animals, pets and lab animals'.

In mid-February 2017 a blog was posted on the OneKind website titled 'Scotland has a hare coursing problem. Here's how to stop it.' The author has a lot of respect for the work carried out by OneKind but they are way off the mark with part of their 'solution'. It is two-fold, and the comments deal with the second part first:

> We're calling for urgent reform in sentencing for hare coursing and other wildlife crimes.

This is already underway in Scotland but will make very little difference. The report of the Wildlife Penalties Review Group recommends an increase in the maximum level of fines and imprisonment, but those convicted of hare coursing to date have rarely received anywhere near the current maximum level. That said, the review group's report gives some short-term solutions:

> Recommendation 2: Use of impact statements: That the use of conservation/ecological impact statements and animal welfare

impact statements is put on a more systematic basis than at present. This might initially be done on an administrative basis with the prosecution seeking these as a matter of course and where appropriate, from either SNH in the former case, or a vet in the latter case.

The value of impact statements in wildlife cases submitted for prosecution cannot be overestimated. In hare coursing cases it will assist the court in its sentencing options if in each case it is made aware through an impact statement that the brown hare is classified as a Priority Species in the UK Biodiversity Action Plan because of its relatively low numbers. The court should also be made aware that poaching, which includes hare coursing, is one of the UK wildlife crime policing priorities because of the volume of criminality.

It is unlikely that the prosecutor, the sheriff or magistrate will have knowledge of Biodiversity Action Plans or Wildlife Policing Priorities. Neither will most police officers be able to help with this. It is up to the wildlife crime officers to ensure that sufficient information on the rarity of the species that is the subject of crime, the ecological effect of killing them, the effect on human victims (such as farmers in the case of are coursing) or any profit likely to be made, is included in the report or file to the prosecutor. In turn the court can then be made aware of these aggravating factors and sentence accordingly.

> Recommendation 4: That forfeiture provisions are extended and these and other alternative penalties are made consistent across the range of wildlife legislation as appropriate.

Forfeiture and *alternative penalties* are the key terms here. This has just been discussed though there are some clear difficulties in the forfeiture of dogs. In Scotland, the options in kennelling dogs in the period between the incident and conviction have been explored in the past, once in fact at the request of sheriffs keen to forfeit dogs. The costs of kennelling were prohibitive, even when in Scotland the SSPCA agreed a reduced rate to keep the dogs. There were also perceived issues if the dogs escaped or were stolen, or if they needed expensive veterinary care. There was also the matter of whether costs would be met by the police or the prosecutor. If there was a will to do so this these problems could be overcome as it appears to be working well in England. In Scotland it needs a committee of the key players to be formed to revisit this option, which would be guaranteed to make a difference.

So far as penalties are concerned, in the initial stages leading up to a trial where a person has appeared in court from custody or on an undertaking to appear, realistic bail conditions may be able to be applied, which could curtail the accused person being with any dog more than, say, a mile from his house. More recently in wildlife crime cases antisocial behaviour orders have been used with success.

OneKind's first solution to hare coursing returns us to the discussion of extra powers for NGOs:

> The simplest way of significantly improving the situation would be to give the Scottish SPCA powers to investigate wildlife crimes

The investigation of hare coursing is not something that can be undertaken by SSPCA. Most of those involved in coursing are invariably violent. They sometimes attack farmers and would not hesitate to do the same with SSPCA staff.

If coursers are caught in the act or soon after, the following powers are required without warrant:

- Power to arrest or detain
- Power to stop a vehicle
- Power to search a vehicle
- Power to search a suspect
- Power to seize a vehicle
- Power to seize any items used in the commission of the

crime or that may help to prove the crime
- Power to seize dogs (outwith any animal welfare issues)
- Access to land to do any of these things

Most hare coursers that are charged are caught in the act. If they are not, their vehicle registration number is seldom of use since many of them buy and sell cars and are only in possession of a vehicle for a short time. The vehicle is almost never registered to them, may be registered under a false name and address and the insurance, since it often covers their trading in vehicles, does not have registration numbers listed. If the vehicle is not traced at the time but is stopped within a few days the chances are it will have been sold on. Investigation can continue by utilising other methods, usually undertaken by a wildlife crime officer. This generally means a lot of effort sometimes with little outcome.

So unless SSPCA staff were going to be given the same powers as police officers, which we know now they are not, they could not have been able to take on hare coursing. Having said that, in unmarked vehicles and along with farmers and gamekeepers, their use would be helpful as 'spotters' during any operation to catch coursers, and to call in a marked police vehicle if coursing is witnessed or suspected.

Hare coursing is dealt with across Scotland under Operation Lepus. Operations are also under way in England to deal with this much more widespread crime, where the coursers regularly drive over the farmers' fields, sometimes taking gates off or cutting fences to do so. The most widely-known is Operation Galileo in Lincolnshire. In 2012 a team was specifically set up to deal with this problem in the county of Lincolnshire. That year the team reported 76 people for related offences, with eight vehicles seized and six dogs recovered. Coming more up to date, in the last four months of 2016, 156 men were arrested or reported for summons and 15 vehicles were seized. In Norfolk, in September 2017 a drone was used against hare coursers for the first time.

In most parts of the UK brown hares are less common than they were a couple of decades ago. As a UK Biodiversity Action Plan species it seems incredible that it is only in Scotland they have some additional protection under a closed season (1 February to 30 September). This needs to be extended to England and Wales.

PART 2

Raptor Persecution Today – Crimes, Incidents, Observations and Interpretations

In the 1990s, when some police forces started to utilise wildlife crime officers on a full or part-time basis, the true scale of wildlife crime, in particular raptor persecution, began to become apparent – and it was truly shocking. There were a few cases which led to convictions towards the end of that decade, the main reason being that gamekeepers, pigeon fanciers and others had got away with raptor persecution for so long they were blasé and careless. Pesticides were recovered to link a suspect with poisoned birds and illegally-set traps were relatively commonplace. Just as important, when a suspect was interviewed he was likely to admit responsibility for the crime.

Very soon pesticides began to be hidden away from vehicles and buildings that had links with the suspect. Gamekeepers took legal advice from lawyers who were beginning to specialise in defending wildlife and firearm charges, with the result that suspects began to respond with 'no comment' to questions when interviewed by the police. Gaining convictions became more difficult.

In an attempt to reduce raptor crime by education and peer pressure, the author, who in the 1990s and early 2000s was the main organiser of the Scottish Police Wildlife Crime Conference, widened the list of delegates to include representatives from gamekeeping and landowning interests. This received criticism from some quarters, especially from some individuals involved in conservation.

Landowning and gamekeeping organisations were also incorporated into the membership of the Partnership for Action against Wildlife Crime (PAW), a UK-wide government-run organisation that helps statutory and non-government organisations to work together to combat wildlife crime. There were some advantages in having a wider membership and in due course representatives of these organisations were co-opted on to various working groups. Arguably the most relevant of these is the Raptor Group, set up in 2009. This group was established to develop a programme of work to improve prevention, awareness raising, enforcement and intelligence gathering related to crimes against birds of prey. Anticipated outcomes from their participation have been disappointing in that wildlife crime linked to sporting estates has continued, with the poisoning of raptors largely being replaced by illegal trapping. Sadly there has been no noticeable increase in intelligence submitted to the police by those involved in game management. In May 2017, according to an article in *The Herald*, the Scottish Gamekeepers' Association pulled out of PAW meetings because it didn't trust wildlife campaigners.

Despite continuing raptor persecution, some gamekeepers and landowners deserve praise for abiding by the law and for their respect of wildlife. This is much more apparent on low ground estates involved in pheasant and partridge shooting. There is little improvement on moorland where grouse shooting interests prevail; in fact, as some estates intensified their grouse management, raptor persecution became worse, as will be seen in Part 4.

So what were the drivers of this criminality? In the first place there is no doubt that profit for the landowner or person employing the gamekeeper was (and still is) the main factor. The more game birds lost to predators meant less to show over the guns on shooting days. Higher bags of birds or an increase in shooting days meant that the estate would gain financially. But it's logical that if an exceptionally high number of game birds are released it makes the estate the equivalent of a game bird supermarket for predators. It follows that there will be many more predators than normal, despite predator 'control.' Predators of course include those that are protected, especially raptors.

Secondly, it is likely that there is still a tradition or culture engrained in some gamekeepers to kill any creature that interferes with 'their' game birds (even though the game birds, once released, become wild birds and do not belong to anyone). This section of the book gives examples of the widespread killing of raptors and considers some of the common public perceptions of birds of prey.

The RSPB UK Birdcrime 2015 Report

The RSPB UK Birdcrime Report 2015 was published at the beginning of February 2017. It showed a gradual downward trend in all types of raptor persecution, though the annual comparison over five years is too short a period to be conclusive. The reduction is heartening, a small change for the better but nowhere near the end of the road for criminality. As expected, the areas of driven grouse moors were demonstrably the worst. In relation to reported incidents of raptor persecution, Lancashire had 19, North Yorkshire, 40, Scottish Borders 20, Tayside 27, Grampian 23 and Highland 39. These six areas of the UK, all areas of driven grouse moors, had 170 incidents out of a UK total of 519.

In the years from 2010 to 2015 the most insidious method of raptor persecution, the use of poisoned baits, runs respectively from 124, 102, 79, 77, 73, 50. There is less movement in the columns headed 'shooting and destruction,' these being over the same years 243, 211, 210, 178, 197, 196. These figures include the use of traps. It is a pity that the methods of 'destruction' are not separated in the report apart from in 2015, when 16 trapping incidents were recorded. It will be interesting in due course to see figures for the trapping of raptors in 2016 and 2017.

There had been two goshawk incidents in the Peak District in 2013 and 2015 when men appeared at active goshawk nests in the middle of the night, and also in what appeared to be conditions of heavy rain. Suspecting that the nesting goshawks might be targeted, RSPB had set up surveillance equipment to record any illegal activity. In the 2013 incident three of the first names of the men were heard as they spoke with each other. Since their motive was almost certainly to get rid of goshawks that might cause them problems with game birds (goshawks would be no problem to a forester or farmer) they are unlikely to have travelled far to the nest and through a combination of criminal intelligence and the use of the details in the firearm licensing department of the local police force there was a potential for them to be quickly identified. This check had probably been carried out but there may have been nothing at the scene to link them apart from a combination of names; they were just black shadows in the video.

Crime intelligence is only of value if there has been a relevant input to the system, which is often a failure of police officers and conservationists alike. The tree had been climbed, and according to French forensic scientist and criminologist Sir Edmund Locard, *every contact leaves a trace*. However halfway up a tree is not the easiest place to carry out a scene of crime examination.

In the 2015 incident four shots were fired, presumably into the nest. The men could be seen scouring the area underneath, presumably to remove any evidence of dead birds of cartridge cases.

The two cases demonstrate how difficult it is to show that a crime against birds of prey has been committed and reinforce the view that the crimes discovered are indeed only the tip of the iceberg.

In a further case, in February 2015, a gamekeeper, Neil Gordon Wainwright of Norbury, Shropshire pleaded guilty to two pesticide offences and the insecure storage of ammunition. He was fined £500 with £115 costs. The circumstances leading to this were that RSPB Investigations staff had found a trap baited with two live quails next to a pheasant pen on land keepered by Wainwright. They installed surveillance cameras, which recorded Wainwright checking the trap, which was of a type sometimes illegally used to catch hawks. The evidence was passed to West Mercia Police and in a subsequent search by police assisted by RSPB the trap and quails were recovered. Wainwright was later interviewed by a West

Mercia police officer and an investigation support officer from the National Wildlife Crime Unit (NWCU). He admitted having set the trap but claimed he was trying to catch rats, stoats and mink!

During the trial, with experts from RSPB Investigations and NWCU available, there would have been no difficulty in proving the trap was set for hawks. Nor would there have been any difficulty for specialist avian vet Neil Forbes in proving that there was a welfare issue in relation to the two quails in the trap.

Following legal submissions about the admissibility of the RSPB video evidence the district judge ruled that the surveillance evidence was disproportionate in this case and dismissed the three related charges. He probably did that reluctantly since he ordered Wainwright to cover his own legal costs, telling him he had brought the prosecution upon himself.

This is the second case that has failed due in part to the archaic term in England of 'trespassers'. The judge said even when 'trespassers', in this case the RSPB staff, acted with the best motives that did not allow their conduct to be 'unfettered'. There may have been another option to gain the evidence required through a proprietary liquid contaminant which adheres to hands and clothing when touched but is invisible except under ultra-violet light. This method may have been accepted by the court.

'I Would Shoot All These Bloody Eagles!'

The following story is an example of how bias against birds of prey still exists even amongst people whose employment is completely unaffected by them. No doubt the media makes a contribution to this.

In February 2013, while visiting a local farm shop, the author met a lady he hadn't seen for a while. They chatted, and a few minutes later her husband appeared. The author was introduced to him as Alan Stewart, the retired wildlife crime officer from Tayside Police. They shook hands and the ensuing conversation went along these lines:

'Yeh, wildlife crime. I can think of some different types of wildlife crime.'

'Oh, what is that?'

'It's all these bloody eagles that have been released.'

'Do you mean the ones that have been poisoned or shot?'

'No, it's the bloody lambs they are killing. It's scandalous that all these birds have been released here.'

'But white-tailed eagles are native to Scotland. They're being released because of the fact that they were exterminated by farmers and gamekeepers. They have a place in Scotland and the release project is righting the wrongs of the past.'

'I would shoot all these bloody eagles. Farmers can hardly make a living for them killing their sheep and lambs, it's a bloody scandal.'

At this point his wife piped up, 'Yes, it does seem a shame for the lambs.'

Author: 'Many of the lambs taken are already dead. There was a study done on North Uist that demonstrated that. They do take live lambs but the majority of the lambs they take have been still-born or have died.'

Eagle Man on High Horse: 'It's not right at all. The whole bloody lot should be shot.'

By the stage that anyone listening would be thinking it was this clown who should be shot, his wife, who by this time was maybe contemplating contacting the League against Cruel Sports piped up, 'It must be terrifying for the lambs to be carried away.'

Indeed it must be but nothing about how terrifying it might be for a mouse or a bird to be caught by a cat, a water buffalo pursued by a pack of lions and eventually suffocated, or the guts torn out of a zebra by a pack of African hunting dogs or hyenas. Ignorance can be bliss, but it can also promote misinformation and prejudice, and condone crime, which damages our wildlife and environment.

There was no sense in continuing a conversation with this idiot – or his wife – neither of whom would be likely to know a gimmer from a tup or a blackfaced sheep from a north country cheviot.

What they collectively knew about farming could probably be written on the back of a matchbox, but it didn't stop the man spouting forth in such detrimental terms about a subject he knew damn all about.

The anticipated pleasure of coffee and cake had evaporated, but the brief meeting demonstrated that every effort should be made to change the biased or anthropomorphic view some have on predators and prey.

The Shocking Bludgeoning of Two Buzzards

The bludgeoning of two buzzards in 2013 by Colin Burne of Winters Park, Penrith, on land managed by a private shooting syndicate in Whinfell Forest, near Penrith, Cumbria, must have outraged all who saw the video. Though there have possibly been more brutal crimes, especially in relation to badger baiting, the dispassionate manner in which this gamekeeper dispatched the two unfortunate buzzards caught in a crow cage trap was sickening. It seemed as if this was an everyday occurrence for him. A man of 64, how many times during his life as a gamekeeper will this scene have been played out. It is something we will never know, but the fact that he pleaded guilty to killing five buzzards prior to this incident tends to suggest that it has been a regular occurrence.

The magistrate would have been shown the video footage of the incident and when Burne appeared for sentence on 8 July 2013 he would be desperate to impose a jail sentence. It was claimed that Burne was in ill health, and a 70-day jail sentence, concurrent on each of three charges, was imposed, but was suspended for 12 months.

Few wildlife crimes have had as much media coverage as this one. It probably sets back the work of decent gamekeepers as much as has any incident where a bird of prey has been killed or a cache of pesticides recovered. Since it was an English case it was unlikely that any relevant game management organisation in Scotland would comment. Disappointingly, though not unexpectedly, there seemed to be no condemning press release from the National Gamekeepers' Organisation, which represents gamekeeping in England and Wales.

This was a case where video footage of the incident was captured by the RSPB, who then reported the matter to Cumbria Police wildlife crime officer PC Helen Felton. RSPB regularly and effectively employ the use of covert video surveillance in England with crime committed against birds of prey, but this is a tactic not normally accepted by the courts in Scotland. In July 2013 the environment minister announced several measures in Scotland aimed at reducing and dealing with wildlife crime. One paragraph of his announcement was of particular interest:

> The Lord Advocate has instructed the specialist prosecutors in the Wildlife and Environmental Crime Unit to work with Police Scotland to ensure that law enforcement utilises all investigative tools at their disposal in the fight against wildlife crime.

The difficulties in utilising covert surveillance, both for the police and for NGOs, is discussed in detail in Part 4 of this book. Despite the Lord Advocate's words, unless the term of imprisonment for wildlife crimes committed on sporting estates is increased to three years or more it is hard to see what else the police can do to obtain the relevant authority to carry out covert surveillance on 'private' land.

Lastly, had vicarious liability been available in England as it is in Scotland, this may well have been an ideal case for the police to investigate and make an example of those higher up the chain of command.

'Keepers Urged to Report Unscrupulous Landowners'

This was the headline in *The Courier* of 8 January 2014. The article is based on an interview with a retired gamekeeper Colin Gair, who is not afraid to speak his mind publicly.

The article begins, 'Gamekeepers are being urged to contact police if they are asked by landowners or tenants to use illegal poisons to protect grouse stocks.' To landowners and tenants should be added sporting agents and head gamekeepers of course, and the illegal methods used should not only be the use of poisons but include any other method of killing of protected species. In principle this is a sound idea, and if the advice was followed it would immediately have a dramatic effect in reducing wildlife crime committed on grouse moors.

It must be acknowledged that not all landowners want their staff to break the law. If the landowner is forceful enough in his or her direction of staff then they take heed. It reverses the risk of being fired for *not* killing birds of prey to being fired for doing so. There are also keepers who have sensibly asked what the policy is on birds of prey before they take the job. In effect there are three categories of employer/employee relationship: those employers who direct their employee to break the law; those who expect the law to be broken despite a useless written contract not to do so – in essence a 'get out of jail free card' for the employer – and those who will not tolerate the law (or at worst certain parts of the law) to be broken.

In the first category, reporting the illegal instructions of an employer (be it landowner, sporting agent or headkeeper) to the police *could* result in a prosecution, but normally these instructions are passed on a one to one basis and corroboration of this, crucial to a conviction in Scotland, could be hard to establish. It may, however, alert the police to a rogue employer of whom they were not formerly aware, though in truth most are already well known. Nevertheless it is almost certain that the landowner or agent would have in force documentation that would safeguard him against prosecution, and if there is any 'fall guy' it would be the gamekeeper. Gamekeepers should always bear in mind that their loyalty to an employer is only reciprocated when it suits the employer.

There are few precedents to whistle-blowing by gamekeepers, and unfortunately much of the game management industry is so defensive against criticism that the whistle-blowers are unlikely to find another gamekeeping job. If game shooting interests are really serious about changing their current negative image then employees reporting management is an area on which they should concentrate, showing support and encouragement rather than exclusion.

In the second category, when law-breaking is promoted by a nod and a wink, there is no evidence against the employer which would ever allow a case of knowingly causing or permitting the offence to get to court. If the gamekeeper happens to be convicted the employer has been known to pay the fine. Depending on the public outcry and the amount of peer pressure the gamekeeper may have to be sacked. Management is still untouched or untouchable. Until recently…

Though vicarious liability is not a magic bullet, by mid-2017 there have been two convictions. In the first case, after his gamekeeper had been convicted for poisoning a buzzard, the landowner was fined £675. This could by no means be considered a hefty fine, but under cross-compliance rules he later had to repay £66,000 of his single farm payment for the year of the offence. In the second conviction, a gamekeeper was convicted of trapping a buzzard in a gin trap. His employer, who runs a game farm, was fined £3,200.

Cross compliance is a term used to refer to the requirement for farmers to comply with a set of statutory management requirements (SMRs) so that they can qualify for a full subsidy payment. SMRs are related to animal and plant health, public, animal and environment welfare. Breaches of the SMRs, which include in certain circumstances the killing of raptors, can mean that all or part of the subsidy for that year is withdrawn. The withdrawal of the subsidy is the remit of DEFRA or of Scottish Government Rural Payment Inspections Directorate (SGRPID), often acting on information supplied by the police.

The legislation, along with the convictions, should act as a deterrent but there remain some incredibly pompous landowners and sporting agents who don't consider the law applies to them. They may well finish up in jail, as they deserve. Just a pity that in England the Conservative government shies away from any wildlife legislation that puts landowners at risk.

In the last category – law abiding employers – indications are that the numbers are slowly increasing. This may be due to the risk of vicarious liability or the realisation that the course of criminal conduct carried out in the name of game management over many decades is no longer acceptable and has brought shooting, at least in Scotland, to the brink of being licensed. There is no need of any reporting to the police since the employee is protected by the employer's stance. This may be the only category where the gamekeeper can sleep at night free from worry of an early morning visit from the police with a search warrant.

It has been recommended for years that gamekeepers make contact with the police when they become aware that a neighbour is breaking the law. It has worked in part (a very small part), with the information given able to be used as intelligence, though never where the witness is prepared to give a statement and if need be go to court. We still have a long way to go and, were it to be acted upon, Colin Gair's plea would take this a step further. If one landowner or sporting agent were to be convicted – and possibly jailed because of their position of authority, plus the fact that human life, not just that of wildlife, is at risk – that would be the biggest step forward ever taken in this sorry saga.

Red Kite Poisonings in Easter Ross

There will be few who do not utterly condemn the poisoning of red kites and buzzards that took place in March 2014 near Conon Bridge in Easter Ross. A total of sixteen red kites and six buzzards were found, most of which were shown to have been poisoned. Some folks, without any evidence whatsoever, are automatically pointing the finger at shooting interests. Police, as professional investigators, need to be much more circumspect and keep all options open. Policing experience of the poisoning of birds of prey on farmland shows that in similar cases the offender may well be a gamekeeper, but could also be a farmer, a farm employee, a pigeon fancier or simply a butcher, baker or candlestick maker who has responsibility for a small shoot and operates mostly at weekends.

In the Conon Bridge investigation, one of the worst poisoning incidents in recent years, it is baffling as to why the police made a press appeal a day or a couple of days before their first search of farm premises. Common sense dictates not to give warning to a suspect of intended or likely police action. Further, in the early stages of the investigation there was no use made of the National Wildlife Crime Unit, either for intelligence purposes or for the assistance of their Scottish investigative support officer, one of the most experienced officers in Scotland on raptor poisoning issues. The information is that they did not even use their own most experienced wildlife crime officer. These were very strange decisions.

Comments on at least one blog asked, 'Do we know what the poison is?' By 'we' it is assumed the questioner meant the public, and of course at this stage of an investigation the public don't need that precise information. To release information specific to any crime while the investigation is live can potentially have fatal consequences for the case. As an example, if premises are broken into by a particular means and, when the suspect is caught, he makes an admission to the police describing this means of entry, a fact that would only be known to the person who carried out the crime, that would be crucial evidence. If in the meantime details of this specialist method had been published, either by the media or in social media, the suspect could then say that this is where he obtained the information, not because he had been the criminal involved.

It is because of these potential pitfalls that police are often reticent to make many crimes public knowledge either until after a conviction or until all avenues of investigation have been explored with negative result. In some crimes, including wildlife crime, there can be exceptions. Examples in wildlife crime may be where there are no obvious lines of enquiry such as where a bird has been found injured, possible from shooting or from having been in a trap, and may have moved some distance from where the offence took place. This is an ideal situation for a press release as soon as the bird is found. It means that a witness *may* come forward, plus it puts the crime in the public domain with minimal risk to a conviction. Another reason for an early press release is if there is a real risk to the public – or even pet animals – through traps set in the open or poisoned baits believed to be set out in an area regularly frequented by the public. In many other circumstances it is often better for the police to keep their powder dry until after initial investigations and searches have been completed.

Despite wildlife crimes in extensive rural areas being challenging to bring to a successful conclusion in court, we have in Scotland a network of extremely experienced police officers and prosecutors. It is much more common now for these incidents to be treated as exactly what they are: another crime. That there is a specialist aspect to their investigation makes them little different to several other types of criminality where painstaking investigation, the use of forensics and sometimes the use of partners' experience is often the key to a conviction.

But failure to utilise more specialist wildlife crime officers and the NWCU in this investigation are major errors of judgement.

By the spring of 2017 no one had been charged with the poisoning incident at Conon Bridge. In Scotland the Wildlife and Countryside Act 1981 has a time bar for prosecutions, which must be commenced within three years of the discovery of the crime. The suspect is now safe from prosecution under this legislation. Wildlife crime, in some circumstances, could be prosecuted under common law, which has no time bar. The relevant common law crimes of conspiracy or culpable and reckless conduct (culpable and reckless conduct is explained shortly) are unlikely to apply in this incident.

The Sledmore Poisons Case and the Pesticides Involved

In December 2012 RSPB Investigations recovered a dead buzzard on the Sledmore Estate in Humberside that had been poisoned by the banned pesticide aldicarb, one commonly used in raptor persecution in England and Wales, though not so much in Scotland. The police carried out an investigation and recovered a number of pesticides that were linked to the possession of the recently retired headkeeper, Derek Sanderson. Two of these pesticides proved to be aldicarb, and carbofuran, probably the most commonly abused pesticide and by far the most commonly abused in Scotland in recent years despite being banned in 2001.

Not only did Sanderson have these two carbamate-based pesticides, but also had a pesticide that had been banned well before carbofuran: mevinphos. This pesticide, usually found under the trade name Phosdrin, is one that was sometimes recovered in Tayside in the early 1990s. While the first two are extremely dangerous they are in granular form, making them slightly less risky to handle than mevinphos, which is in liquid form. It is without doubt the most dangerous and frightening pesticide involved with the poisoning of wildlife, when a spillage on to the skin or even inhaling the fumes could kill.

In the 1980s a Tayside gamekeeper was found dead at his home after handling mevinphos. It seems he got some on his hands and somehow it was then transmitted to his lips with fatal consequences. Another Tayside keeper admitted to have been using mevinphos and related the story that as he was driving his landrover he thought the window was steaming up but in fact it had been his eyes glazing over. He had immediately stopped and washed his hands and face in a burn, which he thinks possibly saved him. A third Tayside gamekeeper was admitted to hospital with hallucinations after using mevinphos. While he was in hospital he thought his dog was having pups under the hospital bed, then the dog was walking along the ceiling. He fled from the hospital and tried to swim a nearby river, almost drowning in the process. These examples, all from illegal use of this pesticide and all from just the one Scottish area, show how deadly this chemical is and how seriously its use – or even its possession many decades after it was banned – should be treated.

Not content with having three deadly pesticides, the fourth one found on the Sanderson search was strychnine. This is a white crystalline chemical that was used extensively for poisoning moles underground before it was also banned in 2006. Like the carbamates, a few granules are enough to cause death. This substance is less commonly used to kill birds of prey but has been encountered in the poisoning of domestic animals such as cats and dogs. Like the earlier poisons, the victims have a horrendous death, with muscle spasms eventually causing the heart and lungs to seize up. In Scotland there are likely to be circumstances with the use or even the storage of these chemicals where the Crown may consider the common law crime of culpable and reckless conduct, which has the potential to take a suspect to one of the higher courts: sheriff and jury or High Court.

Though there seems to be no legal definition for culpable and reckless conduct it is generally seen to be reckless conduct that results in, or is likely to result in, the serious injury or death of a person. The setting out of a rabbit, pigeon or venison cube baited with one of the most-deadly pesticides may well come into that category. It is a huge gamble by the perpetrator, who could well find himself in the High Court; a court that has no limit on penalties in common law cases.

Examples of past cases of culpable and reckless conduct have included:

• Selling glue sniffing kits to children

- Throwing an item off a flyover to hit a vehicle below
- Leaving an item on a railway line
- Organising a rave in a dilapidated building that was at risk of collapsing on the crowd of revellers

One of the more recent cases relates to a person charged with recklessly spinning a car on a public road.

The fifth and last pesticide recovered by the police in Sanderson's arsenal was alphachloralose. This is generally a white powder that kills victims by lowering the body temperature so that they die of hypothermia. It is the safest to handle, but nevertheless is illegal to use apart from by trained pest controllers for pigeons or small mammals and in formulations of generally about 7% purity. When used illegally it is usually found in almost 100% purity and there is little doubt that this would be the case with the sample recovered.

So we are dealing with some incredibly deadly substances here, not only to wildlife but to humans. It is always difficult for the police to make the link between a victim of a pesticide having been killed by the same pesticide as found in someone's possession, but the question must be asked as to why this man had a whole range of pesticides that have never had any legitimate use in game management yet have traditionally been used to poison wildlife on shooting estates. Was he trying to collect the whole range as someone would collect stamps or postcards? That's fanciful. It would be extremely ingenuous not to believe that Sanderson has been using these chemicals for illegal purposes for many years, nevertheless this was not a charge that was proved to the court.

The case eventually came to court in May 2014. The charges for which Sanderson was convicted related to the storage of these five chemicals. Returning to the value to the court of impact statements discussed earlier, would these have been submitted in this case in relation to the effects of the different pesticides involved and the length of time that their use or possession has been banned? It seems unlikely in view of the penalty: Sanderson received six month's conditional discharge (in other words there would be no penalty provided he stays out of bother for six months), and a £15 (that's fifteen pounds) victim surcharge.

A Bad Time for Raptors

The early autumn of 2014 was a bad time for birds of prey. At the end of September a peregrine was found dead in the grounds of St Columb's Cathedral in Derry. The bird, which was popular with locals, became the subject of a police investigation to establish the cause of death and in due course, if death was as a result of a crime, who committed the crime. Suspicions are high that the bird was poisoned. It had previously used St Eugene's Cathedral, also in the city, where it had feasted on pigeons. It was reported in the Derry Journal that the city's pigeon racing fraternity had called for it to be removed from St Eugene's, claiming that its killing sprees are costing members thousands of pounds each year. This would immediately provide the police with a possible motive for the bird's death.

The first port of call could have been to run the bird through a scanner either at a prison or airport. This gives a first-class result, very quickly and free of charge to the public purse, of whether the bird has been shot. The results are almost as good as a vet's x-ray and can even be photographed or a print-out obtained and used in court.

If the bird has not been shot, a post mortem examination would normally be carried out by a veterinary pathologist, which might show the cause of death as due to natural causes. If this examination is inconclusive or appears to indicate poisoning, samples from the gullet and liver in particular would be taken and sent for examination for pesticides. Depending on the pesticide involved the veterinary pathologist may be able to see traces in the gullet, which could be sufficient to allow the police investigation to get under way.

Detecting the person responsible for all raptor persecution incidents is a challenge for the police; this one more than most.

Next, on 2 October, was the welcome news that Allen Lambert, a gamekeeper on the Stody Estate in Norfolk, had been convicted of the killing of ten buzzards and a sparrowhawk. The birds were found to have been poisoned, most with the extremely toxic banned pesticide mevinphos, and Lambert had been found in possession of containers of mevinphos and aldicarb along with needles and syringes. The conviction was as the result of a joint investigation by the police, NWCU, Natural England and RSPB.

If comments attributed to the magistrate are true, a degree of blame was being directed towards Lambert's employer, who had allegedly been lax in the training of Lambert in using legitimate chemicals. This case must yet again make a solid argument for England and Wales to incorporate vicarious liability into their legislation. It is not the complete answer but is considerably better than what is currently available for police, prosecutors and courts to work with.

It is most unusual for there to be sufficient evidence to convict a person of the actual poisoning of wildlife. Most convictions are for the possession of pesticides only, normally with insufficient evidence to link the poisoned baits or victims to the person involved. There have been many investigations with poisoned baits and victims recovered, traces of the pesticide involved recovered in vehicles, gamebags, knives and on suspects' clothing, yet still insufficient to get a case to court. The magistrate would be well aware of all of this, and also that this was hardly a one-off incident. It's a fair bet that during his lifetime Lambert will have killed hundreds of birds of prey and probably other protected species that he has seen as a threat to game birds.

When Lambert appeared for sentence the month following his conviction the judge commented that it was the worst poisoning case that had ever taken place in England. In relation to Lambert's employer he said:

> Those who employ gamekeepers have a strict duty to know what is being done in their name and on their property. They also have duty to ensure their gamekeepers are properly trained and capable of keeping abreast of complex laws relating to the use of poisons. In other industries, employers as well as the employee could be facing prosecution in such cases and I hope therefore that this case can serve as a wake-up call to all who run estates as to their duties.

In this statement the judge couldn't have given a clearer message to the Westminster government to put vicarious liability on the statute books. Rather disappointingly Lambert was sentenced to 10 weeks' imprisonment which was suspended for a year. He had to pay prosecution costs of £930. Under cross-compliance rules Stody Estate lost 75% of its year's single farm payment, which would equate to around £180,000.

Some Good News for Raptors in Glenesk

In early July 2015 there was at last some good news regarding birds of prey in Glenesk, Angus. Millden Estate in Glenesk has seen the recovery of poisoned birds of prey over the years, the most notable being the recovery of a satellite-tagged golden eagle, Alma, in 2009, however a news story in *The Courier* was heartening.

On Gannochy Estate at the bottom of the glen a red kite's nest was found by a trainee keeper, who made the headkeeper aware. The headkeeper, Dave Clement, contacted RSPB to report the find and arrange for the two chicks to have wing tags fitted. The author has been on Gannochy Estate on several occasions by invitation and has watched a variety of birds of prey, including a goshawk, which Dave said he had seen several times. An arrangement was also made through the Gannochy Estate landowner for an estate visit by Roseanna Cunningham, in her role then as Minister for the Environment. Nesting kestrels and barn owls were the highlight.

The other news in the article was that a young golden eagle on

Invermark Estate, the estate at the top of Glenesk, had been ringed by members of the Angus Raptor Study Group. The ringers were driven to the nest site by headkeeper Garry MacLennan. Invermark has two pairs of golden eagles, and Garry is quoted in the article as saying,

> Last year we actually had three eaglets from one nest which is very rare. An abundance of white hares probably helped. There are always peregrine and merlin nests too.

The proliferation of mountain hares is also really good news. Invermark is another estate the author has visited many times by invitation of the late headkeeper Fred Taylor, who was pleased to show off one of the pairs of eagles and a peregrine nest site with the female on guard. It is rather surprising that in January 2013 a tree on that estate containing a white-tailed eagle nest was felled. Regrettably the crime remains undetected.

'Bad' Buzzards and Sparrowhawks

In early August 2016 a letter appeared in *The Courier*. It was in response to an article by nature writer Jim Crumley on the lack of legal protection for the wild beaver population in Tayside. The first half of the letter, headed 'Farmers also love nature', sounded quite promising but not so the second half:

> Once again, I was annoyed after reading the article from Mr Crumley (2nd Aug) in which he says farmers and keepers would rather kill everything inconvenient that moves rather than give nature time and peace.

> Mr Crumley, we are farmers, and most evenings my husband and I have a walk round the fields to look at the cattle, and it would not be the same if it was not for the wildlife around us.

We will see maybe a deer and of course all the different birds – that is, the ones a buzzard or sparrowhawk haven't killed.

Why can't you see, Mr Crumley, that there is good and bad in wildlife, just as there is with humans.

We think just as much, believe it or not, of our wildlife as you do, but we as farmers see at first hand the devastation some species can cause, both to our own animals and to nature.

Of course sparrowhawks will kill small birds; that is what they eat. Buzzards will take young ground-nesting birds such as lapwings and oystercatchers; that is part of their diet. In terms of evolution this is nothing new. Predators have killed and eaten prey for thousands of years. Lions eat zebra, orca eat seals, dolphins eat salmon, peregrines eat pigeons, blackbirds eat worms, blue tits eat greenfly, bats eat midges. What is comparatively new is interference by the most dangerous predator: man.

While we may not necessarily kill other creatures to eat them, we destroy their habitat: worldwide, the pollution of seas and rivers and the destruction of forests; in the UK the ripping out of hedgerows, enlargement of fields, spraying of crops, cultivation and rolling of fields. And many of these actions are carried out by farmers, the occupation of the letter-writer who is complaining of some birds being killed by predators! Predators, as inferred in the letter, are the 'bad wildlife' which, as the letter writer reckons, take farm stock and native species (though she'll maybe excuse buzzards taking rats or rabbits).

Most farmers deserve respect as producers of our food, and their job seems to get more difficult by the year, but they must realise that modern farming methods have killed off far more farmland birds than predators do. Anyone who is at least 60 will have witnessed first hand the change in farming and the rapid disappearance of skylarks, grey partridges, lapwings, yellowhammers and corn buntings.

Thankfully this is being addressed to some degree by some farmers who are taking practical measures to ameliorate these losses, sometimes at their own expense, but it will be a long time before wildlife on farmland returns to what it was even half a century ago.

Could the letter-writer be one of these conservation-minded farmers? Somehow I doubt it.

Fenn Trap Appeal

In October 2016 a noteworthy appeal by police appeared on Twitter. The appeal was for information from any member of the public who may have had knowledge related to a pole trap discovered on farmland in East Devon. The trap was a Fenn trap set on top of a post beside a pheasant pen. It was photographed by the police in situ, set and ready to trap any bird that landed on it, most likely a bird of prey of some sort.

So far so good, but instead of taking possession of the trap and having it tested for DNA or even fingerprints which could lead to the identification of the person who set it, the officers left it there, intending to collect it the following day. The next day, however, it was gone.

It is hard to believe that Devon and Cornwall Police, a force with a first-class record of investigating wildlife crime, (a) left a trap in the set position where it could well have caught a victim, and (b) missed out on an opportunity to gain good forensic evidence.

Having photographed the trap, presumably with corroboration, there would still be sufficient evidence to convict in relation to its use, but having left the trap set exposes the officers at any trial to awkward and embarrassing defence questioning that could have been avoided.

It is probable that the officers attended in uniform, maybe even in a marked vehicle, which is hardly discreet. It matters less if all the evidence can be gathered at that visit, but if further visits are required, either to the scene or to a suspect, it is prudent to work on the basis that the suspect is likely to be aware of the initial visit. Despite this apparent faux-pas, from the photograph of the trap and the set-up described, with a bit of work and good interviewing the police may still have managed to get a case to court.

The RSPB Birdcrime 2016 Report

Bringing us right up-to-date, on 1 November 2017 the RSPB published their *Birdcrime* report for 2016. During that year they had recorded details of a total of 81 confirmed raptor persecutions in the UK. These comprised:

- 40 confirmed shooting/attempted shooting. Victims included two hen harriers, seven peregrine falcons, 14 buzzards and 11 red kites.
- 22 confirmed poison (pesticide) abuse incidents. Victims included 13 buzzards, four red kites and two peregrine falcons.
- 15 confirmed trapping incidents. Victims included two buzzards, two kestrels and one peregrine falcon.
- One confirmed nest destruction incident involving a buzzard nest.
- Three confirmed 'other' persecution incidents.

Of those 81 incidents:
- 53 (65%) occurred in England (in line with the five-year average of 54).
- 13 (16%) occurred in Wales (higher than the five-year average of eight).
- 9 (11%) occurred in Scotland (lower than the five-year average of 27).
- 6 (7%) occurred in Northern Ireland (slightly lower than the five-year average of eight).

Breaking down methods or persecution, these are –

Shooting and destruction of birds of prey:

2011	2012	2013	2014	2015	2016
213	210	177	189	196	160

Poisoning of birds of prey:

2011	2012	2013	2014	2015	2016
102	79	79	73	50	53

In line with what will follow in the pages of this book, the league table – or more accurately, the table of shame – for confirmed raptor persecution during 2012–2016 is:

North Yorkshire	54
Scottish Borders	22
Powys	22
Aberdeenshire	20
Norfolk	19
Down	8
Angus	17
Derbyshire	16
Cumbria	14
Highland	13
Perth and Kinross	12

So raptor persecution continues to be an ongoing issue. In fairness the number has fallen substantially in Scotland, though as reported earlier poisoning now seems to have been replaced by trapping. The slight improvement in Northern Ireland is also welcomed. What has to be borne in mind, of course, is that these figures only show the incidents discovered and which can be confirmed as a crime. Many more must remain undetected and unreported, particularly those that occur in remote and private areas.

Comments following the release of the *Birdcrime 2016* report were interesting to say the least, particularly in *The Times*, a newspaper normally very defensive of landowners and shooting interests. It quoted the National Gamekeepers' Organisation, representing gamekeepers in England and Wales:

> very few stupid keepers and landowners [broke the law]. These dinosaurs sully the good name of modern shooting, putting at risk its long-term future. The only effective solution lies in changing the collective mindset of those involved.

The Scottish Gamekeepers Association, also featured, saying that it had expelled six members in five years over alleged wildlife crime but that the majority of its 5,300 members were law-abiding:

> In Scotland, the greatest issue we wrestle with is the lack of access to legal measures to solve species conflicts. We feel this would have more impact than any other measure to prevent wildlife crime.

This seems to imply that licences to kill raptors would be preferable to their members working within the law.

The editor of *Shooting Times* claimed that some young gamekeepers felt pressured by their employers to kill raptors, and concluding 'If the shooting community refuse to admit it, the future for our sport could be bleak'.

Tim Bonner, head of the Countryside Alliance, said that historically gamekeeping techniques had devastated hen harrier populations but that there was a 'generational shift' taking place towards better conservation. 'It's our role to encourage that change of attitudes.' (Another strange statement. As the pages of this book will show there is nothing 'historical' about the devastation of hen harriers; it is very much ongoing and substantiated by the regular loss of satellite-tagged harriers over grouse moors.)

Thankfully, and at long last, a frank and honest statement from the UK's largest shooting organisation, the British Association for Shooting and Conservation (BASC). BASC is by far the most rational and reasonable of the organisations representing shooting and game management. Christopher Graffius, acting chief executive, said that killing the raptors to protect game birds was a 'fool's bargain' that his members had to stop or risk their sport being banned. He said in a letter to BASC members there were 'criminals among us' who risked 'wrecking shooting for the majority. All of us need to realise that the killing of raptors is doing us no favours. It risks terminal damage to the sport we love.'

He further stated that expelling members who were convicted of raptor persecution was not enough, and that shooting needed a cultural shift to make such people pariahs.

> Peer pressure is a powerful force in shooting. We must make clear that wildlife crime has no place in our community.

In contrast, demonstrating how unlikely it will be for England and Wales to have improvements in legislation that might curb raptor persecution, Jim Shannon MP (DUP, Strangford, NI), one of the bedfellows of the Conservatives, was quoted in Hansard (2 November 2017) as asking Parliament,

> The number of birds of prey across the United Kingdom of Great Britain and Northern Ireland has risen astronomically to the detriment of songbirds. The Department for Environment, Food & Rural Affairs does occasionally grant licences to cull birds of prey, but many country people and landowners who want to avail themselves of such licences in order to achieve a balance in the countryside find the process to be off putting. Indeed, sometimes

they cannot get a licence. There are too many birds of prey and too few songbirds and mammals, so will the Leader of the House grant a debate on that or call for a statement from DEFRA?

It's appropriate to end this chapter with a quote from the blog of freelance journalist James Marchington who specialises in writing about Britain's wildlife, the countryside and fieldsports. The blog is entitled 'Poisoned eagles and the Osborne connection':

Another eagle falls victim to illegal poisoning. The story is reported in the *Guardian*. And once again the name of Mark Osborne is not far away. Osborne is known for his ability to take a poor grouse moor and turn it around, vastly increasing grouse numbers – and the moor's value – in a few years. Of course it could be coincidence, but several moors run by Osborne have been at the centre of illegal poisoning scandals in recent years.

Local keepers are hopping mad at the damage done to shooting's reputation. And there's no doubt where they are pointing the finger.

Just a few greedy estates are trashing the damage done to shooting and undermining all the good conservation work done by the vast majority of shoot managers in Britain. Surely we are best paced to weed them out?

This blog was written in 2009. Sadly the weeds are still thriving.

PART 3

Partnership Working and the Use of Experts

In criminal investigations the best evidence is all important, and some of this can – and indeed does – emanate from witnesses more skilled than the police in aspects of wildlife and ecology.

Police officers are experienced in enforcing the law, particularly utilising interviewing skills. Many interviews of suspects are tape recorded or even videotaped, with consideration of the questions and strategy carried out in advance. Wildlife crime officers have the additional – and not insubstantial – knowledge of wildlife laws. This does not make them experts in wildlife, though a few officers, mainly through their outdoor pursuits, have extensive experience of a narrow field of wildlife and ecology. This limited number of officers may be considered experts, for instance, on specific species such as raptors or badgers. More so than in most specialisms of policing there is a need for experts from various organisations to be brought on board during many wildlife crime investigations. Most experts are used for identification of species but other assistance is required to explain the ecology or distribution of the species, a cause of death, the effect of a particular pesticide and many other areas of expertise.

Few wildlife crime investigations come to court without the involvement of experts. An example might be the identification of birds' eggs, which is normally carried out by RSPB Investigations staff. Evidence of bird species of conservation concern is also available from the RSPB. In badger-related cases a badger expert is normally required (Scottish Badgers, Badger Trust, badger consultants), with the same requirement in cases involving bats (the Bat Conservation Trust, Scottish Natural Heritage, English Nature etc); deer (the British Deer Society or SNH), seals and cetaceans (the Sea Mammal Research Unit, Whale and Dolphin Society); hare coursing and post-mortem examinations (the Scottish Rural College); poisoning (Scottish Government Rural Payments Inspections Directorate or Science and Advice for Scottish Agriculture); traps and snares (Science and Advice for Scottish Agriculture or the British Association for Shooting and Conservation); salmon poaching (water bailiffs); cruelty or animal welfare cases (vets or RSPCA/SSPCA). In one case where a sand martin colony was flattened the police had probably the foremost expert in the UK in sand martin breeding come to the court to give evidence. His mere presence at the court seemed to be enough to make the accused person change his plea to guilty before the trial started.

These partnership working arrangements mainly relate to Scotland, but similarly apply in other parts of the UK. We have the additional benefit in Scotland in that all wildlife or environmental crime or cases of animal welfare have the involvement of a team of specialist prosecutors.

This chapter demonstrates the success of some of these partnerships. It also points out where other potentially beneficial partnerships still need some work to come to fruition.

The LINK Report. Partnership Working – Or Not!

Scottish Environment LINK is the forum for Scotland's voluntary environment organisations. Over 35 member bodies represent a range of environmental interests with the common goal of contributing to a more environmentally sustainable society.

The police do not always get it right and from time to time could make a better job of certain wildlife crime investigations. The LINK report, rather disparagingly named *Natural Injustice*, was a review published in February 2015 of the enforcement of wildlife protection legislation in Scotland. Unfortunately, it set back rather than improved partnership working. It consistently and unfairly criticises police, NWCU, COPFS and the courts, yet unbelievably was completed without any consultation with any of these organisations. In addition, the report which tracks the progress of wildlife crimes committee during the period 2008 to 2013, does not take account of improvements in practices since that period.

Some sections of the report are well worthy of comment.

> The four areas of wildlife crime are under-recorded and the standard of information that is recorded is generally inconsistently collected which limits its usefulness. (*Natural Injustice* p2)

Almost all crime is under-recorded, though I accept that recorded crime against wildlife in rural areas, particularly uplands, shows only a small proportion of what is actually taking place. Without consultation with the police and without seeing crime reports, how does the report author know the 'standard of information' recorded? When crime reports are raised they are updated on an almost daily basis with new aspects of the investigation. This allows the officer in charge, supervisors, crime management and any other officer with an interest to see the state of the investigation, details of any suspects, searches, evidence recovered, lines of enquiry still to be carried out and details of anyone charged.

> At least 27 wildlife crimes (18.2%) did not result in a follow-up investigation and were effectively ignored. It is feasible that as many as one third of reported incidents were un-investigated (*Natural Injustice* p2)

This is supposition, but the true position could have been established through the crime reports discussed – or the lack of such a report. A missed opportunity for accuracy through not consulting Police Scotland. There are long-established complaints procedures with the police. I wonder how many of these anecdotal incidents that allegedly caused dissatisfaction were made the subject of a complaint.

> Of the follow-up investigations that did occur, LINK respondents considered just over one third (35.1%) to have been conducted satisfactorily. Criticisms included delayed police response times (sometimes as long as several months from the initial incident report) leading to the disappearance of evidence, delays exacerbated by un-trained police wildlife crime officers and a lack of seriousness with which senior police officers treat wildlife crime, failure to apply for search warrants, failure to conduct covert searches, poorly-targeted and/or restricted search efforts, the premature disposal of evidence prior to toxicology examination and a chronic failure to communicate with partner agencies either as a result of police under-resourcing and/or politically-motivated deliberate exclusion policies. *(Natural Injustice* p3)

The statement LINK respondents 'considered' again shows supposition, which could have been verified through consultation with Police Scotland and reference to crime reports. I am not disputing that in some cases some of these criticisms may be justified but lack of consultation with Police Scotland makes them little more than conjecture. There may have been a valid reason, for instance, for not applying for a search warrant or restricting a search. Reasons would be documented on the crime report. I do agree that some senior officers do not treat wildlife crime seriously. This is often in middle management and requires direction from executive officers.

A further paragraph states

> LINK assists communication between member bodies, Government and its agencies and other sectors within civic society.

There was a distinct lack of communication in the compilation of this report.

'The Ideal Investigative Process of a Hypothetical Wildlife Crime Incident'

Before providing a critical assessment of current wildlife crime enforcement procedures, it is perhaps useful to set out LINK's view of how the investigative process ought to proceed, based on LINK members' primary experience of investigations and incorporating some of the relevant recommendations made in the *Natural Justice* Report. (The Natural Justice Report, published in 2008, is the result of a joint inspection by Her Majesty's Inspectorate of Constabulary for Scotland (HMICS) and the Inspectorate of Prosecution in Scotland (IPS) into the prevention, investigation and prosecution of wildlife crime in Scotland).

The following scenario is a hypothetical (but not uncommon) wildlife crime incident with a brief narrative of the ideal protocol for each stage of the investigative process.

SCENARIO: A member of the public witnesses a group of men with dogs and spades, leaving a wood known to house a badger sett. One of the men, who lives locally, is known to the witness. The witness then finds a dead badger close to the sett. The witness, who wishes to remain anonymous and is nervous about speaking to the police, reports the discovery to an NGO.

The follow-up options, depending on the available evidence, are a search under powers given to the police under Section 19 of the Wildlife & Countryside Act 1981 and/or a contemporaneous or subsequent application to the sheriff (via the procurator fiscal) for a search warrant to allow entry to dwelling or lockfast premises for the purpose of obtaining evidence. The crime could be indicative of a continuing pattern of offending so the follow-up action needs to take place as quickly as possible. (*Natural Injustice* pp 23–25)

The assumption is made that the NGO to which the incident is reported relayed the information to the police timeously so that a recovery of the dead badger and any other evidence can be made. The principles in the investigation process as given in the LINK report are sound and indeed in most cases this is exactly the way a badger-related investigation would be carried out, with the most likely partner involved being Scottish Badgers.

An inaccuracy that would bar a prosecution is their reference to powers given to the police under Section 19 of the Wildlife and Countryside Act. LINK has quoted the wrong legislation. Powers of search and the application for a warrant would be under the Protection of Badgers Act 1992, not the Wildlife and Countryside Act. The crime may indeed be part of a continuing pattern of offending, but if any earlier incident has been dealt with by SSPCA the intelligence on this is unlikely to have been passed to Police Scotland and if that is the case would not be available to the police or to NWCU to include in any intelligence package. This is a major failing and would be a potential impediment to investigation.

LINK report comment on an investigation into raptor poisoning:

> In both cases the inability to undertake a comprehensive search for evidence to link the crimes to a particular individual or estate meant that there was no further follow-up. Had the first search warrant been issued it may well have prevented the deaths of the two buzzards and second white-tailed eagle. Why both search warrants were refused, in spite of the overwhelming supporting evidence, is utterly bewildering. (*Natural Injustice* pp 33–34)

This comment relates to a case in which I was involved in 2008 and where the procurator fiscal refused the search warrant applications.

Nevertheless what is not recorded here are other innovative lines of enquiry, which I cannot discuss further in a public forum, which were carried out by police wildlife crime officers and RSPB Investigations. These were unsuccessful but the comment fails to show that the investigation continued despite the refusal of search warrants.

> In addition to inadequate communication between the police and partner agencies, there was widespread concern amongst respondents about the timeliness and quality of publicity relating to wildlife crimes. Clearly, for operational purposes, public information about a follow-up investigation should be restricted until such time that the suspects are aware that a crime has been discovered... (*Natural Injustice* pp 34–35)

Publicity, and the timing of such, is always up to the officer in charge, often under guidance from Crime Management. My own view, subject to any prejudice to the investigation, is that the earlier a press release is circulated the better. That a witness may come forward is unlikely but the press release serves to keep wildlife crime in the public eye. It has been my opinion for some time that the publicity on wildlife crime should be led by the police and not by a non-government organisation that may have had involvement. I regularly see RSPB leading a press release on raptor persecution. This is not their fault as the press sometimes contact RSPB rather than the police. It is up to the police to change this practice, submit a press release and encourage RSPB or other relevant NGOs to augment it.

Some respondents' concerns quoted in the LINK report:

> 'My concerns are with the lack of resources and the changing police force in Scotland, the very light sentencing (if any) and the turning a blind eye of the judicial system (old boys club).'

'I am concerned about the apparent reluctance of the prosecuting authorities to take action against certain offenders. In my experience I have found the police on the ground to be taking wildlife crime seriously; the problem seems to be rooted higher up the chain somehow. The underlying structure of society with powerful landowners dictating policy and pulling the strings will continue to be a problem for wildlife and habitats.'

'Why isn't more use made of the SSPCA in investigating wildlife crime? Can we be assured of the objectivity of police investigations especially in the smaller, rural communities in which police and their families have to live? In short, why do the owners of driven grouse moors and their agents seem to enjoy a privileged relationship with those who enforce the law and those who administer justice?'

'It is well known that the large majority of the shooting estates are operating well outside the law when it comes to so-called predator control, (we all know what that means to a gamekeeper), rampant poisoning, trapping and shooting of raptors and carried out in the full knowledge that the law will do nothing to stop them even if they are caught at it.'

'However, there is sometimes a certain lack of trust in wildlife crime officers who are shooters themselves and who are very friendly with gamekeepers.' (*Natural Injustice* pp 66–75)

Some of these comments appear to imply corruption, which is a serious allegation. While some wildlife crime officers, fiscals and sheriffs may be less experienced or less competent than others, in my 50 years of being involved in policing I have never witnessed nor suspected corruption. I am not saying that there are no – or have never been – some dishonest police officers, but police forces have always gone to great lengths to get evidence to get rid of them as quickly as possible. The real problem in investigating wildlife crime on shooting estates is the lack of evidence to identify the suspect. It is at least as frustrating for police officers and prosecutors as it is for LINK members. In relation to the last comment regarding a police officer who may also be a shooter, that officer is in an ideal position to gather intelligence but must exclude himself from any investigation where he is friendly with a suspect.

In some parts of Scotland dead raptors that have been found and reported are taken by the police to airports for x-rays to establish if they have been shot. I feel that there should be enough Government funding to support alternative x-ray locations where experts in this field can examine the raptors, without fear of contamination to the evidence and also so that there is better continuity of evidence if a case ever reaches court'. *(Natural Injustice* p 67)

I must take issue with this comment, which is possibly well-meaning but erroneous. I initiated the use of scanners in airports and prisons in Scotland to save the public purse from expensive vets' bills for x-rays and also to have x-rays carried out when vets' practices may be closed, such as on a Sunday. Before a victim is taken for examination for poisoning, it is helpful to x-ray it first to see if it has been shot. Some birds that have been poisoned have also been shot on an earlier date, though the shot has not been fatal. The x-rays can be photographed and have always been accepted by the fiscal and by the courts. They show shotgun or airgun pellets perfectly and also show traces of lead left by a bullet that may have passed right through the victim. There is no 'risk of contamination', and no effect on 'continuity of evidence'. If the fiscal thinks that an x-ray by a vet might better show the cause of death the victim can be further examined, but this has never been necessary.

With the Police being so short of personnel and resources to deal with raptor (and other wildlife) crime it would seem sensible to recruit the assistance of SSPCA. By giving the SSPCA extra powers it would substantially increase the efficiency of the Police in enforcing wildlife crime law. (*Natural Injustice* pp 67–68)

In relation to extra powers and more involvement from the SSPCA, I read an interview of Mike Flynn, one of the senior staff of SSPCA, in *The Courier* around the beginning of February 2015. In the interview, Mike stated that SSPCA staff was at full stretch. In view of that comment it seems unlikely that they would be able to take on an expanding role. Even if SSPCA staff were granted additional powers to widen their animal welfare investigations to include the investigation of wildlife crime where there was not an animal in distress it is perfectly possible that both they and the police could be working on the same investigation unknown to either organisation. (In any case, the request for extra powers was refused).

I am concerned by the lack of input by NWCU into priority cases (except CITES). NWCU is a nonentity in Scotland, with Investigative Support Officer now just an office boy.

From what I can gather the NWCU seem to be totally focused on gathering 'intelligence', partnership working, and designing 'apps'. What a waste of time they are. Do they do any fieldwork or investigations? Obviously not otherwise we would never have heard the end of it. Talking about partnerships, they don't seem to put into practice what they preach. Do they work in partnership with RSPB and SSPCA and the expertise available in these organisations? One final observation but a very important one is the collation and recording of wildlife crime statistics. Obviously there are a lot of raptor persecution incidents and it is vital that we record each and every one. Otherwise there would not be a problem of persecution. So who should record such incidents?

Knowing the Police way of recording incidents, they will not record a crime unless they can prove that there is in fact a crime. This is the basis of all forms of their crime recording, whether it is assault, robbery, vandalism etc. Wildlife crime will be no different. So there will be numerous wildlife incidents not recorded as they, the Police, cannot prove that there is an actual crime'. (*Natural Injustice* p 68)

These are obviously comments from someone who knows nothing about the NWCU. Again it is supposition and conjecture which could have been explained through consultation. Like Police Scotland and COPFS, NWCU was left out of the consultation process. The NWCU only has one investigative support officer in Scotland. He is involved in almost every major case – not just CITES – provided he is asked. In one major raptor investigation (the Conon Bridge poisonings) he and the then force's most experienced wildlife crime officer were not asked to become involved. Had they been present, subsequent failings in the investigation may have been averted. So far as involving RSPB, SSPCA or any other partner, this is not the remit of the NWCU, but is the remit of the investigating police officer. One of the main functions of the NWCU is the collation and utilisation of wildlife crime intelligence. SSPCA submit no intelligence to NWCU! The comment states: 'Obviously there are a lot of raptor persecution incidents and it is vital that we record each and every one.' The police do not record an incident as a crime unless it can be substantiated as such. That is common sense. Men coming out of a wood with terriers and a spade is an incident, not a crime. A badger sett that has been dug out is a crime. However 'incidents' are recorded as intelligence and there is a clear failure of some non-government organisations, including Scottish Raptor Study Groups, in passing details of incidents to Police Scotland or to NWCU. Some of the NGOs may even have signed up to intelligence-sharing protocols with the police yet have submitted little or nothing. Missing intelligence can cause an investigation to fail.

In recent years the activity has been reduced to tiny numbers of (egg) collectors. Jail sentences handed out for repeated offences seem to have persuaded almost everyone to abandon the behaviour. Much of this can be attributed to the success of Operation Easter – a campaign led by the police, but also using the expertise provided by the National Wildlife Crime Unit, and the RSPB. It continues to target egg collectors by sharing intelligence and monitoring their activities, as well as raising public awareness of suspicious behaviour. This excellent example of good partnership working began some 17 years ago, (in 1997) and, alongside the imposition of custodial sentences for the worst offenders, has had the result of reducing the numbers of active egg thieves to a tiny rump of obsessive individuals. *(Natural Injustice* p 34)

This operation has been successful because of the availability of imprisonment plus the real risk of being caught due to all UK police forces and RSPB working together. I have run Operation Easter for almost all of the time since its inception and I am pleased it was thought worthy of positive mention in this report. The principles of the operation would not work across the spectrum of wildlife crime. It could be successful with badger baiting and badger digging but would not be suitable for raptor-related crime.

Operation Easter, ongoing since 1997, is a police-led operation very much in partnership with RSPB Investigations and aimed at combatting wild bird egg thieves. All police forces in the UK are involved. In 2011 the ownership of the operation transferred from Tayside Police to NWCU.

In the twenty years of the operation known active egg thieves have been reduced from around 130 to a handful, and even some of those now concentrate their egg collecting outside the UK. Though the operational strategy cannot be discussed it is successful because the criminals involved have to travel to commit the crime. The same could be said for badger diggers, who would fit the criteria of Operation Easter perfectly, though unfortunately there are many more badger diggers than there are (or were) egg thieves. The operation could assist with badger-related crime if it were to be taken on and developed by the police, but would be dependent on a heightened awareness by police and any relevant NGOs to submit badger crime-related intelligence and to do so timeously.

Criminals who kill raptors, whether they be gamekeepers, farmers or pigeon fanciers have little need to move off of the land on which they work or where they reside. It is difficult to devise an effective way to catch and convict them; better to devise a means of preventing them by the imposition of sanctions that make them stop in their tracks. An Operation Easter equivalent, therefore, would not work.

The following are recommendations made by the LINK report which I comment on as appropriate.

Recommendation 1: Government and the wildlife NGOs should urgently discuss, agree and introduce measures to address under-recording; improve the standards for reporting; and introduce consistency across all areas of recording wildlife crime.

There is no doubt that the recording of wildlife crime needs to be improved to allow full extent of this criminality to be realised. This should be addressed by the Scottish Government and Police Scotland.

Recommendation 2: A three-tier classification system should be introduced for use by all agencies, assigning a widely agreed and accepted 'confirmed', 'probable' or 'possible' category to each wildlife crime case, and grading information according to established police systems.

A crime report should be completed for every confirmed wildlife crime. This can also be done for a 'probable' crime, which can be deleted if there is subsequent evidence that the incident turns out not to be a crime. It is much more difficult under an official system to record 'possible' wildlife crimes, which in effect are no more than incidents at that stage. Nevertheless there are other means by which to record these incidents, namely by the submission of intelligence to Police Scotland.

> Recommendation 3: The Wildlife Crime Annual Reports should include, henceforth, an evaluation of the full extent of wildlife crime in Scotland.

> Recommendation 4: Police Scotland should review the full complement of Wildlife Crime Liaison Officers (WCLOs) and Wildlife Crime Officers (WCOs) in terms of the basic number of whole-time-equivalent officers dedicated to this area of work. The basic complement dedicated to this area of work as its priority should be stated publicly, and used as a baseline – to be increased if it proves ineffective.

I would like to see a full-time wildlife crime liaison officer (the title given by Police Scotland to the police officer co-ordinating wildlife crime in each Division) in each of the 13 Divisions and for all to be able work together as a unit under a sergeant or inspector. If they had a Scotland-wide remit this would address the issue of an urgent wildlife crime not being dealt with there and then because of the absence of the local WCLO or WCO(s).

> Recommendation 5: The complement of WCLOs and WCOs should be rigorously targeted by Police Scotland at the areas where wildlife crime is known to be greatest. Consideration might be given to the feasibility of establishing a national wildlife crime rapid response unit, to be comprised of multi-agency partners who could respond to reports of serious wildlife crime.

The targeting of resources is an operational procedure regularly carried out by the police and to use this tactic in respect of wildlife crime would be no different. It would be up to the officer in charge of the investigation as to whether partners would be involved at any stage of the investigation. However there is merit in many cases in the police having the assistance of partners experienced in particular fields. It is a system which I regularly utilised, particularly requesting RSPB Investigations staff for land searches.

Recommendation 6: Police Scotland should agree a wildlife crime strategy, in consultation with the wildlife NGOs. The strategy should be intelligence led and carefully targeted at the areas of criminality.

The most successful investigations emanate from good intelligence. It is disappointing that, with few exceptions, particularly Scottish Badgers, RSPB, Bat Conservation Trust, RSPCA and League against Cruel Sports, little or no intelligence is submitted to Police Scotland or to NWCU by NGOs. As one of the recommendation in Natural Justice a wildlife crime reduction strategy was prepared by PAW Scotland in 2008. It can be found at http://www.gov.scot/Topics/Environment/Wildlife-Habitats/paw-scotland/Resources/Reports/WildlifeCrimeStrategy

Recommendation 7: Police Scotland should improve the basic wildlife crime training modules for all police cadets at the Scottish Police College and ensure compulsory, on-going training for all appointed WCLOs and WCOs.

There are no longer police cadets as they were phased out around 1970. Training on wildlife crime (and some other aspects of policing) for recruits has been reduced or discontinued as part of the curriculum at the Scottish Police College due to funding issues. Annual training for WCLOs and WCOs has been ongoing both at the Scottish Police College and within forces for nearly 20 years. For the past decade or so it has also included training along with specialist prosecutors. Consultation with the police by LINK could have established this.

> Recommendation 8: The Crown Office and Procurator Fiscal Service (COPFS) should urgently investigate why such a high percentage of cases fail to be prosecuted, and review arrangements for the allocation of its resources and training.

Any response to this should come from COPFS.

> Recommendation 9: Follow-up investigations of wildlife crime by Police Scotland should be carefully monitored by COPFS and the expertise of partner organisations should be consistently and fully used. Results of investigations should be fed back to complainants.

In more complex investigations COPFS is involved from the outset. It makes sense that in some wildlife crime investigations expertise of partner organisations should be utilised, though in some cases the additional resources, if any, the police may utilise has been directed by COPFS. I agree totally that complainants should be updated. This was sometimes a failing of mine and probably is one of the most common failings in policing, though not for any reason of keeping the complainant out of the loop.

> Recommendation 10: The Wildlife Crime Annual Reports should include cumulative figures for prosecutions brought and the resultant rate of convictions.

I agree, and the Wildlife Crime in Scotland Annual Report 2015 now has much more detail.

> Recommendation 11: Stiff sentences should be asked for by

COPFS to allow for proper consideration of deterrent effect by the courts, and the consistency of sentencing should be carefully monitored by the appropriate authority.

It has never been the practice of prosecutors in Scotland to attempt to influence the sentence passed by a sheriff. Good use of conservation/ecological impact statements and animal welfare impact statements, as recommended in the 2016 Wildlife Crime Penalties Review report, would allow a sheriff to fully understand the effect of the crime and to sentence more appropriately. These should be considered by the reporting officer as crucial.

> Recommendation 12: The Scottish Government should urgently institute confidence-building measures and improved partnership working between Police Scotland, COPFS and the wildlife organisations, with clear instructions that the latter are not to be excluded from the process of investigation or prosecution, and their expertise and information sources should be properly and fully utilised in the fight against wildlife crime.

Confidence-building measures and improved partnership working may be more difficult considering Police Scotland and COPFS were not consulted during the preparation of the LINK report! The input from partners is important for the success of many investigations and in fact relatively few wildlife crime investigations are carried out by the police without advice or assistance, at some stage, from at least one partner. This input is sensible and does not need 'instructions'. The report appears to want to dictate the terms of an investigation through NGOs, which happens in no other aspect of crime investigation.

> Recommendation 13: If the partnership approach is to continue, the Scottish Government should commission research to assess the true extent of the different types of wildlife crime in Scotland and

remove any group tainted significantly by an association with any area of wildlife crime from PAWS.

This is an unsubtle hint at removing land management groups from PAW Scotland. This recommendation discounts the value of members of these organisations that are law-abiding and keen to reduce wildlife crime. Police officers are regularly 'Piggy in the middle', being accused on one hand by land and game management of siding with RSPB and Scottish Raptor Study Groups, and on the other hand accused by RSPB and SRSG of taking sides with land and game management. In effect police officers are – or should be – unbiased. Those involved in game management who commit wildlife crime are a disgrace and need to be dealt with. By the same token members or supporters of NGOs who try to discredit the police, COPFS and the courts as being corrupt or involved in conspiracies are no better and do the investigation of crime a great disservice.

Recommendation 14: The Scottish Government should immediately remove poaching from the PAWS remit and deal with it as a distinct and separate matter.

This recommendation links in with the previous one as hitting out at land management. Deer poaching, salmon poaching and hare coursing are the most commonly reported wildlife crimes, with one of the main issues being animal welfare concerns.

Recommendation 15: The Scottish Government should ensure that preventative measures are assessed rigorously – and targeted effectively.

This has not been done previously but will hopefully begin to be addressed by the targeted withdrawal of general licences and through the outcomes of the independently-led group to be set up in 2017 to look at the environmental impact of grouse moor management practices.

Recommendation 16: The Scottish Government should consider how wildlife crime might become a material consideration within the land reform programme, and how it can be made into a major element within the statutory Land Use Strategy.

Recommendation 17: The Scottish Government should consider how any wildlife crime directly connected to land use on a specific piece of land might lead, consistently, to the withdrawal of subsidies associated with land ownership – and should publish, in its annual wildlife crime reports, a summary of Single Farm Payment and other penalties imposed as a result of wildlife crime.

Recommendation 18: The Scottish and UK Governments should consider how any wildlife crime directly connected to a land use on a specific piece of land might lead to the withdrawal of all fiscal privileges associated with land ownership, as an additional sentence available to the courts.

These last three recommendations are valid and may also be considered by the independently-led group already mentioned.

It is telling that the Lord Advocate in place at the time of publication of the LINK report refused to meet LINK members to discuss the report. I doubt it was any better received by Police Scotland, NWCU and the specialist prosecutors within COPFS.

Freshwater Pearl Mussels Joint Investigation

Though this case study does not relate to raptor persecution nor bear relationship to any form of shooting or game management it is worthy of inclusion as it is one of the best examples of agencies working together on a wildlife crime incident.

The freshwater pearl mussel (*Margaritifera margaritifera*) is one of the longest living invertebrates, living in rivers that have extremely good water quality and capable of living for well over 100 years. Its range has shrunk considerably due to various pressures including pearl fishing, pollution and river engineering. Even though the mussel is absent in many rivers where formerly there was a healthy population, Scotland may now hold approximately half the known remaining breeding populations in the world and therefore has a critical role in supporting its continued global survival. The Scottish Natural Heritage (SNH) national survey in 2000 and further survey work shows that of 208 watercourses known to have been occupied 100 years ago, pearl mussels are extinct or about to become extinct in approximately two-thirds. In Scotland, only 71 watercourses are known to continue to support freshwater pearl mussel populations that show evidence of breeding. These rivers are of the highest global conservation value for freshwater pearl mussels, with the River Lyon in Perthshire being such a river. It is therefore of truly international importance.

It is against this background that in late August 2010 the then Tayside Police, together with staff from Scottish Natural Heritage and Scottish Environment Protection Agency began an investigation into what was likely to be the reckless killing or injuring of freshwater pearl mussels, or damage or destruction to their place of shelter. The case concluded in Perthshire Sheriff Court in March 2013.

The police were first made aware of the incident on 23 August 2010 by SNH, who in turn had been notified by SEPA of extreme silting of the River Lyon in Highland Perthshire caused by work on a mini hydro scheme in the Inverinain Burn, which runs into the River Lyon. Though SEPA officers were carrying out their own investigation under the Water Environment (Controlled Activities) (Scotland) Regulations 2005, there was very much the potential of a separate but parallel police investigation as it was almost certain that the freshwater mussel population of the River Lyon would have been badly affected.

It was learned early in the investigation that recent surveys had confirmed the presence of pearl mussels including juveniles in the River Lyon. On 24 August, to establish to what extent this population had been affected, Constable Steve Band and the author, along with Iain Sime and others from SNH and SEPA staff, including their investigating officer, Brendan Craig, visited the River Lyon. They were devastated by what they found: a thick layer of fine silt several centimetres deep covered the bed of the river from the Inverinain Burn downstream for hundreds of metres. Iain and his SNH colleagues spent hours in the freezing river searching for and photographing evidence. They found colonies of large mussels that were not syphoning properly because of the silt, and concluded that the smaller immature mussels would be completed covered and effectively suffocated. It was an ecological disaster, albeit localised.

The police role here was considerably easier. Steve and the author photographed what they could from the bank and noted what was being found and photographed by the SNH staff in the river. Even in August the water would be freezing cold and the SNH folks were to be commended, each with one hand and arm, just about to the shoulder, almost continuously immersed in water, while the other hand held the glass-bottomed bucket that gave them a clear view of the bed of the river.

Constant rain after the initial search, with the consequent rise in river level, delayed further attempts to obtain evidence, and no further examination could take place until 12 October. The SNH staff again found a large percentage of the mussels were still closed and therefore not filter-feeding. They may in fact have been dead. In undisturbed conditions nearly all mussels would be open and filter feeding. It was Iain and his colleague Nicky McIntyre's opinion that, as a result of the silt, mussels had been killed and injured and the habitat occupied by them had been damaged.

Separate cases were submitted to the specialist wildlife and environment procurator fiscal, Tayside Police reporting wildlife offences and SEPA reporting pollution offences. The accused were two companies and their directors. The procurator fiscal raised a prosecution for pollution offences and included in those charges the narrative of causing damage to the river bed and killing and injuring freshwater pearl mussels. Shawater Ltd, who designed the project, pleaded guilty to permitting the pollution to occur, and at Perth Sheriff Court on 18 February 2013 was fined £4000. The specialist wildlife fiscal, Tom Dysart, told the court that it remained unclear how long it would take for the mussel population in the River Lyon to recover, if at all.

Sentence was deferred on Alan Smith, a director of sub-contractor A & C Construction Ltd, and Charles Kippen, also a director of A & C Construction Ltd and a director of Chic Kippen & Sons, who both admitted causing pollution which killed and injured pearl mussels. On 19 March, Kippen was fined £5000 and Smith £6000, though Smith's fine also took into account another pollution-related incident at Dalmally, Argyll.

The case provides a classic example of effective partnership working, with each of the various partner agencies bringing their specialist skills to the investigation, and with consultation with the Wildlife and Environmental Crime Unit (WECU) prosecutor from the outset.

The Nature and Use of Corvid Cage Traps

In 2015 SNH commissioned a report to assess the nature and use of corvid cage traps in Scotland since several had been found very obviously set for birds of prey. The field work was carried out by Science and Advice for Scottish Agriculture (SASA) and the Game and Wildlife Conservation Trust (GWCT). The project was overseen by a steering group of representatives from RSPB, BASC, SNH and Scottish Government. The report was published in late 2016.

The main concern was on how the field workers would view the use of the two newest traps, the Larsen mate (clam) trap and the Larsen pod trap.

Most designs of traps for corvids are used legally, unfortunately they also have the capability of being used illegally by those who might wish to catch birds of prey. A real concern about the clam trap was that a large bird such as a buzzard is likely to be caught with its wings up in the air and sticking out of the top of the trap. A mammal such as a fox or badger might also be caught round the neck if it reached in for the bait. Since the attention of the Scottish Government and SNH was drawn to the illegal use of clam traps they have been restricted to being used with baits of eggs or bread only. The general licence also states that the trap must be securely pegged down so that it cannot be removed either by an animal caught in it or a predator. It also stipulates a maximum size of the trap and that the trap must not shut tightly along the majority of the length of the meeting edges. Stops could be used to good effect in preventing complete closure and the consequent trapping of wings or a bird's head.

In relation to the catching of raptors as by-catch during the trial the vast majority were buzzards. Observations found that buzzards were only caught in traps with meat baits and/or decoys. This applied not just to the clam trap but to all of the traps tested. An occasional tawny owl was caught in a trap with eggs or bread, and a sparrowhawk was caught in a trap with a carrion crow as decoy. In this case the raptor, which mainly takes live birds, may have entered to try to catch the crow. It may be that the owls were trying to catch mice at the bread bait.

For the 2017 general licence the use of meat bait in Larsen mate (clam) and pod traps has been permitted provided that those intending to do so register their intent in advance and provide SNH with a return of non-target captures. There must be doubts that true returns will be made since evidence of substantial non-target catches are likely to result in the return to bread or eggs bait only.

In addition, during 2017, in conjunction with Police Scotland

and Scottish Government, a code of practice for corvid trapping is to be developed. Also under consideration during 2017 is a discussion with Police Scotland on a revision of the trap registration system. SNH may take ownership of the system and, as in snaring registration, ensure that the register shows the operator of the trap rather than the owner.

That so many agencies had involvement in this work made the process and results more acceptable. It is unfortunate that none of the changes will prevent abuse or misuse of corvid traps by those determined to do so. Crow cage traps and Larsen traps that have been in legal use for many years are still sometimes used illegally. Some Larsen mate traps and pod traps will no doubt be abused in the same manner. If, as suggested, individual operators of the traps can be established through a better licensing system than is currently the case, with a presumption in law that the person licensed is the operator, that will make enforcement much more effective and at the same time act as a deterrent.

An increase in time allowed by police managers for their wildlife crime officers to investigate trapping offences (or better still an increase in full-time wildlife crime officers) plus more use of the current power of SNH to suspend the use of a general licence would not go amiss.

Birders Against Wildlife Crime

Birders against Wildlife Crime (BAWC) was formed in 2014 by five bird watchers in England. The aim is to encourage the thousands of men and women who go bird watching to be aware of wildlife crime, to make field notes of it if possible, and to report suspicions to the police. The following is from their website:

> BAWC is a simple idea – and, some will say, not actually a new one. Wildlife charities have been asking the public to keep an eye out for wildlife crime for a long time.

We're approaching things slightly differently though.

First off, we're birders talking to birders. And we understand that part of the problem in tackling wildlife crime is that the laws surrounding wildlife crime are very complex: many of us don't know what exactly is or isn't a wildlife crime, what we should do and what details we need to record when we see a crime, and who we're supposed to report that crime to.

So we're putting together a website and campaign materials that will focus on what we've dubbed 'The Three Rs':
Recognise   Record   Report.

Whether or not the idea is new – the police and the NWCU have been making this request to the general public for many years now – it is good advice. Bird watchers, with their field skills, cameras and binoculars are as well placed as anyone to witness and recognise the whole range of wildlife crime, from raptor persecution, reckless disturbance of nesting Schedule 1 birds, hare coursing, illegal snaring or trapping, finch trapping, badger digging, poaching, taking freshwater pearl mussels and wild bird egg thieving.

BAWC has gone from strength to strength, with large numbers participating, and it has hosted a popular annual conference since 2015. It was also instrumental in the formation of the hugely successful Hen Harrier Days, held in advance of 12 August, which have increased in number and attendance. In 2017, ten Hen Harrier Days took place across the UK, including in Northern Ireland. Around 2000 people attended in total in a great show of strength of feeling at the fate of hen harriers on grouse moors.

In a true partnership, many more eyes and ears are now focussed on the same objective, making it much more likely that wildlife criminals will have their day in court.

Badger-Related Crime and Forensics

During early March 2015, there were some good convictions in England and Wales for badger-related crime. One particular case came to a conclusion in Dales Magistrates Court in Chesterfield on 27 February and resulted in three criminals in their 20s being sentenced to 12 weeks imprisonment.

Two of the culprits had been caught by police as they tried to flee from the scene of their crime, a badger sett that had been dug and partly back-filled. With the use of thermal imaging equipment and a police helicopter, a third man was found hiding in a nearby field. When they examined the area of the sett, police found locator collars, three shovels and six dogs. Close to the area of backfilled earth they found a badger with its skull smashed in.

With the knowledge of forensic techniques common across a range of crimes committed against humans or property, police seized the men's clothing, which was blood-stained, and submitted items of clothing, the dead badger and the shovels for examination. This was carried out at Science and Advice for Scottish Agriculture (SASA) on the outskirts of Edinburgh. Wildlife DNA work is regularly carried out there by Dr Lucy Webster at SASA on behalf of Police Scotland with considerable success. In this case the DNA on a vest worn by one of the accused and on a shovel were found to be a match, and proved to originate from the dead badger.

In addition to their jail sentence the three men were banned from keeping dogs for life, which is an important part of any sentence involving animal cruelty and something the prosecutor should always be aware of asking the court to consider. Part-way through the investigation RSPCA joined forces with the police, giving the added dimension of their expertise in animal welfare cases.

As this badger-related case came to a conclusion, another was just beginning. Sgt Rob Taylor, wildlife crime officer for North Wales Police, and his team had just finished executing a search warrant on a property in Caernarfon and had seized five dogs.

Hopefully, with advances in investigations available such as the use of thermal imaging, police helicopters and a specialist wildlife DNA service the odds are stacking against badger-diggers. They are amongst the lowest form of criminals and most rightly deserve to be jailed for their crime.

A Snared Badger and the Use of Entomology

In November 2015, a quantity of fly larvae was aged by the Natural History Museum in London, allowing a successful prosecution against a gamekeeper for snaring offences. A badger, still alive, was caught in the snare near Skene in Aberdeenshire and the SSPCA had reported the case to the procurator fiscal. In the dock at Aberdeen Sheriff Court, the gamekeeper involved admitted that he had not checked the snare within the required period – *at least once every day at intervals of not more than 24 hours* – and had also failed to fit to the snare a tag with his identification number issued by Police Scotland. He was fined £600.

Science, in this case entomology, is being used more and more in wildlife crime cases. An earlier case of the aging of blowfly maggots took place around 2001 in a case near Callander in the west of Perthshire. A farmer was investigated by the then Central Scotland Police wildlife crime officer for failing to check a snare within the timescale set out by legislation. Once again it was a live badger that had been caught and the blowfly maggots were aged by entomologists at Stirling University, which showed that they were at least three days old, the minimum period of time that the badger had been in the snare.

Around 2010 Tayside Police tried an innovative method of determining how long a dead fox had been in a snare. There were no maggots on the fox as the season was late autumn but the grass under the fox was yellowing through loss of chlorophyll. The grass was photographed and ten short planks of wood were set out on a grassy area. One plank was turned over every day until the stage was reached when the grass began to lose its chlorophyll. This took three or four days and matched the estimation by the veterinary pathologist of the period of time that particular fox had been dead. Hardly scientific, but effective.

Professionalism in snaring has improved considerably since legislation in Scotland was updated in 2004 and again in 2011, but unfortunately there are still people using snares who disregard the law. Snaring is a legal method of catching foxes, but in both of the above cases not only has the law been ignored by the users but a protected animal has been the victim.

Gas Guns Disturbing Hen Harriers – Reliance on Experts

In the second half of 2015 complaints were made about the use of gas guns on grouse moors in the north of England, allegedly used to prevent hen harriers from settling and nesting. A gas gun is a gun placed in a field, normally by farmers, to keep pigeons (sometimes rooks or geese) off their crops. It fires periodically, scaring the birds off. The newer models are powered by gas, whereas the original variety was powered by carbide of calcium onto which there was a regular drip of water until sufficient gas was built up to cause an explosion. It had the same effect.

The use of gas guns other than on agricultural land is questionable. If they are used on grouse moors, is there really a legitimate purpose for them? The claim is that they are there to disperse flocks of immature ravens. If, however, they are being used with the intention of disturbing hen harriers prospecting for a nest site, what does the law in Scotland say about this?

The first offence, if indeed an offence is being committed, may come under Section 1(1)(bb) of the Wildlife and Countryside Act 1981 as amended.

> *1.- (1) Subject to the provisions of this Part, if any person intentionally or recklessly–*

(bb) obstructs or prevents any wild bird from using its nest
he shall be guilty of an offence.

To prove this there would firstly need to be evidence that a hen harrier nest was present or being built. It is highly likely that this would need to be ascertained by the observations of raptor experts before the use of the gas gun begins, since the birds would be quickly scared off their nest by the continual banging. The presence or building of a nest would also need corroboration, as would the fact that the bird was prevented from using or returning to the nest by the user of the banger. None of this would be unduly difficult to prove, but the crunch comes in identifying the person responsible for the use of the gas gun, and proving that he or she used it to *intentionally* or *recklessly* prevent the harrier from returning.

Since the hen harrier is a bird included in Schedule 1 to the Wildlife and Countryside Act, almost the same elements of proof are required under Section 1(5)(a) of the Act –

(5) Subject to the provisions of this Part, if any person intentionally
or recklessly–
(a)   disturbs any wild bird included in Schedule 1 while it is
building a nest or is in, on or near a nest containing eggs or young;
he shall be guilty of an offence.

Lastly, the police may consider Section 1(5B) of the Act, which reads –

(5B) *Subject to the provisions of this Part, any person who intentionally or recklessly harasses any wild bird included in Schedule 1A shall be guilty of an offence.*

Since the hen harrier is included in Schedule 1A to the Act, this section may be of use if there is no evidence that the hen harrier has begun nesting but there is evidence that a male has been displaying in the immediate area.

Much of the evidence will of necessity be from people who have considerable knowledge of hen harrier ecology, most likely from RSPB or members of raptor study groups. This is a classic case of where the police depend on the knowledge of experts who should be able to convince a court that the bird at issue is indeed a hen harrier, and can give evidence relating to the displaying, mating, nesting and breeding of this species.

So how can it be proved that the person deploying the gas gun is doing so with intent to dissuade harriers from nesting successfully? If the person involved is a gamekeeper, as is most likely the case on a grouse moor, there is no doubt that he or she will have a good knowledge of the places that harriers like to nest, such as in long heather often on sloping land running up from a hill burn. The gamekeeper will have experience from previous years and will most likely have watched a displaying male. Telling this to a court will certainly not be enough to secure a conviction; it must be proved beyond reasonable doubt.

The most likely route to reach the stage of 'beyond reasonable doubt' is for experts such as those mentioned who become aware of a displaying male harrier, a nest being built or a completed nest on land where a gas gun has been used in the past, to contact their local police wildlife crime officer and discuss the situation. Officers (two officers, bearing in mind the need for corroboration) may consider approaching the gamekeeper for the estate, and indeed the estate owner, factor, sporting agent or headkeeper (bearing in mind the offences of knowingly causing or permitting, and vicarious liability) and advising them of the presence of a nest or a displaying harrier. They would also need to be warned that the use of a gas gun nearby is likely to lead to a report for prosecution. At the very least this should be a crime prevention measure.

Cynics may think that this will alert the gamekeeper to the presence of the harriers, but the gamekeeper is on the land every day of the year and will already be aware of the birds. If, after a police warning or advice, a gas gun is deployed (or not removed if already deployed), and the harriers are adversely affected, then at the very least a charge entailing a reckless act may be relevant. If the gas gun is already in use the damage will probably have been done and the warning to the estate may well only be effective for the following year, or in the unlikely event that the bird re-lays in the same area.

Codes of conduct from statutory authorities may assist, but it is not easy to prove that a suspect has read and understood this guidance or advice.

This is a difficult situation but one for early liaison between bird experts and police wildlife crime officers. Any conviction here would definitely require good partnership working.

A Worrying Breakdown in Partnership Working

In the various appendices to the RSPB Birdcrime Report 2015, published in 2017, there were several pesticide abuse cases listed as being investigated by Police Scotland where details of the type of pesticide has been withheld. In Scotland the police have three years from the date of the offence to get a case to the procurator fiscal (less a few months for the fiscal to prepare the case for court). It is common in the investigation of *any* crime not to put specialist knowledge that only the person committing the crime may have into the public domain. In this respect it is not surprising that pesticide details have been withheld, however it is unusual that there are no details at all of four incidents; neither listing the species involved nor the area of Scotland in which the incident took place. There is considerable criticism of Police Scotland for completely withholding all details of certain raptor persecution cases. An explanation of why this has been necessary would help to get the public back on side.

In mid-February 2017 Police Scotland responded as follows:

Primarily, the Police Scotland concern is about specialist knowledge becoming public knowledge in these cases. Police Scotland actually withholds the data from publication in relatively few cases and only after consideration against the agreed investigative strategy for a particular case. If Police Scotland is to make an appeal for information about a bird of prey killing and has chosen not to identify the substance as part of the strategy (or even identify that poisoning was the cause of death) this would be undermined by the identification of the chemical used in a public document. It would not take too much initiative to put the two together and that specialist knowledge tool is lost. A similar argument is equally as legitimate where other modus operandi (MO) are used in this form of raptor persecution.

On occasions, the decision is made not to make an investigation public at all for a variety of reasons (time of year, other oNGOing investigations etc.). Publication of pesticide data or MO by Health and Safety Executive, RSPB or whoever else would ensure that Police Scotland loses control over this tool.

Differences in the legal system in Scotland is also another issue. The time bar for bringing wildlife crimes to court in Scotland is (in most cases) three years from the date of the offence. Police Scotland therefore expect to be able to legitimately withhold information relating to cases for that time period. This argument was supported by a specialist prosecutor from the Crown Office and Procurator Fiscal Service's Wildlife & Environmental Crime Unit who also thought that this was particularly relevant in Scotland because we still have a requirement for corroboration.

Police Scotland cannot speak for the approach taken by forces in England and Wales but our commitment to wildlife crime ensures that we must ensure that we use every tool available and therefore on occasions this will include withholding information about a crime.

Following the police response, a blog on the Raptor Persecution UK site was headed 'Police Scotland intend to withhold raptor persecution crime info for three years'. This heading appears to convey the meaning that none of the data will be released until three years has passed. This is unlikely to be the case and is certainly not the author's interpretation of what was written by Police Scotland. It may be that some of the more sensitive material will be withheld but it is improbable that the police, in each and every raptor persecution case, would withhold all details from the public until the three-year period has passed.

The reason the details are missing remain unknown but some of the readers of the blog are clearly making the assumption that the police are involved in some sort of collusion with raptor killers. Whatever the reason for withholding certain information it will not be for any corrupt purpose. A particularly worrying comment on the saga of the withheld data read,

> ...if anyone finds something suspicious regarding raptor crime, make sure you tweet it and tag in as many people as possible before calling the cops.

The naivety of this comment is of real concern, and the outcome of such action is likely to alert the criminal involved long before any investigation can be made.

The frustration of folks interested in raptors (or in any wildlife for that matter) is perfectly understandable. Their anger when the birds are the subject of crime is justifiable. It is completely proper that Raptor Persecution UK blog should publish details of raptor crime at every opportunity, though the police should generally be beating them to that. Considering the political importance (at least in Scotland) of raptor persecution the police should strive to be transparent and publish relevant incidents at the earliest date possible *provided it does not jeopardise any future court proceedings.* That is unfortunately not always being done and press coverage of this type of crime is often led by RSPB with no quote from the police. Many investigations into raptor crime involve partner agencies, particularly RSPB Investigations. They and others can often add valuable information to a media release but it should be clear that the investigation is being carried out by the police.

It is worth remembering that the police are in support of raptor enthusiasts and are keen for them to be partners in the fight against wildlife crime (as demonstrated in Birders against Wildlife Crime). This is especially so of officers who have been trained in wildlife crime investigation, many of whom have been desperate for years to get suspected raptor killers before a court.

With cases of pesticide abuse there is always a risk to anyone encountering a poisoned bait or the victim of a bait, which makes a media release even more essential. Several years ago a couple of teenage girls picked up a dying buzzard on the roadside bordering Edradynate Estate near Aberfeldy in Perthshire. The buzzard had been sick and the breast feathers were wet. As it turned out the bird had been poisoned by the pesticide alpha-chloralose. Had it been the much more toxic and more commonly used pesticide carbofuran the girls would have been in real danger.

So, partnership working, when implemented, can make an investigation more likely to result in a conviction or can improve legislation or working practices. By the very nature of police work NGOs, as partners, cannot be involved in *every* investigation but some more transparency, where this is possible, is necessary to keep the public on side.

The most effective way of working *for* the public is to work *with* the public.

Operation Manhattan – North Wales Police Badger Crime Operation

It was interesting in early February 2017 to watch the enforcement of Operation Manhattan by North Wales Rural Crime Team. From updates regularly unfolding on Twitter the operation dealt with badger crimes and the associated animal welfare issues of the dogs used in the brutal 'sport' of digging and baiting badgers. From the information in the public domain, three men were arrested on the day of the searches and a fourth has been interviewed. A 'wild' animal, probably a captive fox or badger, was recovered from a locked shed, and 42 dogs were seized.

This was a massive undertaking and was an excellent example of the police working in partnership with other agencies. Running an operation involving many police officers and other staff is a daunting task. For those who are not too acquainted with policing, and some of the difficulties involved, the following is an educated guess at the work that the North Wales Police Rural Crime Team undertook. The team is led by Rob Taylor, recently retired sergeant from the team and now the team manager, and consists of a detective constable on secondment, three constables and three community support officers.

Most police operations are intelligence-led, and the intelligence for this operation may have originated from the police, the National Wildlife Crime Unit, RSPCA, League against Cruel Sports or from any combination of these agencies. Invariably search warrants are required, and these will only be granted by a sheriff or magistrate who is convinced by *current* intelligence that there are reasonable grounds for warrants to be issued. In this operation, it is likely that at least four search warrants would have been required.

Four search warrants mean at least four locations to be searched, maybe even some distance apart. (In a Tayside raptor persecution investigation which the author organised, there were seven search warrants, plus about 30,000 acres of moorland to be searched, though police powers for the land were sufficient and this did not require a warrant). In Wales, this probably meant at least four police officers to each address, assuming they had to be searched simultaneously, which would most likely be the case since word could spread quickly and evidence was likely to disappear. Two of the officers would be involved with each search, probably with the assistance of specially search-trained officers, one of whom would be an exhibits officer (or in Scotland, a productions officer) to log the productions. Two might also be involved assisting at the address but would be available to detain or arrest the suspect if and when that became necessary.

In an operation of this magnitude wildlife crime officers from other forces may be asked to assist, as may investigation support officers from NWCU. In this case dog section officers were on hand as was a firearms unit. The request for their assistance would depend on the intelligence and any background knowledge of the suspects.

It is always important to provide a court with the best evidence possible, so it is likely that the recovery of any interesting items, the dogs and the conditions in which the dogs were kept would also be video-recorded and/or photographed.

In a case like this it would also be anticipated that dogs would need to be examined and probably seized, which would require a vet, who could move between addresses, and possibly two RSPCA inspectors at each address to deal with and remove the dogs.

So, we now have an idea of the considerable staffing required for the job, but of course transport is also required. It would be easy to have a van for each locus and to pile everyone for that address on board. That's certainly not suitable as officers carrying out different tasks are likely to need their own transport as some may need to leave the address before others or even move between addresses. In many of these operations vehicles are hired for the duration of the job. RSPCA would also have their own transport with cages to remove animals, whether dogs, foxes or badgers.

There must be communication between the different teams, and indeed with whoever is controlling the operation, who might be at a police station rather than at any of the addresses. (In the Tayside operation, the author was based in the nearest police station to the operation along with a uniformed inspector – the author had the knowledge but, as a retired police officer, little or no authority, while the inspector had the authority but little knowledge of wildlife crime or associated wildlife or animal welfare legislation). Every team member must therefore know how to contact the other team members. The officer in charge must also be considering the welfare of those in the teams and work out, if possible, how to get some refreshments to them. There are seldom complaints from team members as they are normally so busy they hardly notice that 10 or 12 hours have passed without a bite to eat (in Operation Manhattan some of the officers worked a 17-hour day).

The expense of carrying out an investigation of this magnitude is considerable, though costs are reduced by the involvement of partner agencies, in this case the RSPCA. Nevertheless the cost for police officers alone would be substantial and getting the authority from senior ranks to run the operation is not always easy. Fortunately, in an interesting wildlife crime investigation of this type overtime payments are the very least of the participants' considerations: they just want a satisfactory conclusion and some extra time off in lieu of payment.

The day starts, normally very early, with a briefing by the officer in charge. Every team member must know exactly what he or she has to do and, equally importantly, if there is anything that he or she must *not* do. At the end of the operation it is good to have a debrief, though it is much harder to get everyone back together again as some tasks take much longer than others. The debrief allows important information and intelligence gleaned to be shared. It is also an opportunity to pick up on what aspects of the operation went smoothly and what went wrong, which can inform future operations.

The searches are just the beginning of the operation. Items seized are likely to be dogs, locator collars, mobile phones, computers, laptops, iPods, tablets, photographs, video footage, relevant books and articles on the subject of the search, cages, blood and hair samples, any documents showing ownership of the dogs, home remedies for treatment of injuries and any documentation that might show veterinary treatment. Forensic work on some of these exhibits/productions may take weeks or even months. RSPCA invariably take on the difficult job of looking after the dogs. This would include veterinary treatment, the cost of which is unlikely to be recoverable from the owners of the dogs.

Suspects have to be interviewed. The position with suspects is different in England and Wales compared with Scotland but it would be unlikely, unless absolutely necessary, for the suspects to be kept in custody for the court. Custody cases force the prosecutor's hand into making decisions on whether to prosecute on sometimes limited and hastily-prepared evidence. It is generally better to put a complete case forward once all evidence has been gathered. In wildlife crime cases, the police would normally be in consultation with the prosecutor at an early stage in any case and could be directed appropriately.

It was really impressive that North Wales Police kept the public abreast of the progress of this operation through Twitter. It is yet another aspect of an already busy day for the officer in charge, but is an incredibly clever strategy for garnering public support and information, so important in trying to get a successful conclusion in wildlife crime cases. Most operations of this sort are run equally efficiently; it is just that the public are not aware of them. Full marks in any case to North Wales Police, to Rob and his team and to the other participating organisations. All police forces are struggling financially but others would do well to follow the North Wales Police example of creating an extremely competent and dedicated rural crime team.

In September 2017 four men and two youths appeared at Caernarfon Magistrates Court in connection with Operation Manhattan. Charges included causing unnecessary suffering to a badger during a fight with dogs, failure to provide veterinary treatment for dogs, failure to properly care for dogs, failure to give them water, wilfully injuring a badger, attempting to cause an animal fight to take place, being present at an animal fight, exposing three dogs to risk of injury by fighting them with other animals, keeping premises for use for an animal fight and causing unnecessary suffering to two foxes by confining them in close proximity to dogs.

They pleaded not guilty and, as at November 2017, still await trial.

PART 4

Driven Grouse Shooting:
'A Business Underpinned by Criminality'

The increase in raptor persecution in recent years is inextricably linked with the resurgence of intensively managed driven grouse moors.

In the early years of the 21st century some estates with multi-millionaire owners began to employ sporting agents in order to increase their stock of grouse thus enabling the much more lucrative driven, rather than walked-up, shooting. In driven grouse shooting those shooting are driven to and ensconced in shooting butts, often with two shotguns and a person loading for them. The grouse are driven towards the butts by a line of beaters. Bags of grouse shot in a day can be into the hundreds. In walked-up shooting, which is normally done with the use of breeds of dogs which 'point' and then flush the grouse, only two or three 'guns' are usually involved. They walk through the heather behind the dogs and the day's bag may not reach much more than double figures.

The emergence of intensively managed moors saw the removal of the incumbent gamekeepers, who were replaced by younger, enthusiastic but much more malleable ones, many of whom were from the north of England. These keepers were immediately put on much higher wages than their predecessors, invariably had their living accommodation modernised, were supplied with brand-new 4WD vehicles, but in return were expected to work very long hours. Most of these estates went from having a couple of keepers to having seven or eight.

Typically, double electric fences were erected around the estate and deer and hares were either eliminated or seriously reduced. One of the factors involved in intensively managing grouse stocks is to reduce species which are likely to prey on grouse. It wasn't long before complaints flooded in to the police about illegal practices in relation to the killing of raptors and some species of mammals. These were backed up by the regular recoveries of shot, poisoned or trapped raptors, poisoned baits and illegally-set snares and traps, some holding otters or badgers.

In the effort to increase the estates' profits the law is ignored, discarded as inconvenient. For policing purposes, the elimination of protected wildlife to increase profit could be termed serious and organised crime, and in the words of Logan Steele of Tayside Raptor Study Group, he described driven grouse shooting as a 'business underpinned by criminality'. Logan went on to organise a petition asking the Scottish Government to licence the sport of shooting.

It is worth emphasising that if a landowner *really* does not want the law broken by his employees he or she will instruct them accordingly, and make them aware of the consequences of doing so, which, if it is to be effective, should be immediate dismissal. Until vicarious liability for certain wildlife crimes became law in 2012 (at least in Scotland), landowners and other management levels were almost bombproof. To prove that any person '*knowingly* caused or permitted' the offence (the killing of a raptor) to take place is extremely difficult. Many employers and managers hid behind employees, sometimes paying their fines if they were unlucky enough to be caught and convicted, but with almost no risk of gaining a penalty and subsequent criminal record themselves. While vicarious liability may never be easy to establish, it has increased the risk to employers, and should thereby have some deterrent effect.

In the majority of cases those convicted of any form of raptor persecution (a) have no previous record, and (b) the raptor involved is usually one of the more common species, such as a buzzard. This makes it very difficult for a court, much more used to dealing with regular offenders and with serious violence, dishonesty or drug-related cases, to hand out a sentence of imprisonment. Having said that, there have been cases where imprisonment might have – maybe even should have – been on the cards, but without knowing all the facts, and any mitigation put forward by the defence, it can be hard to take issue with a court verdict.

Police officers investigating crimes have to be objective and can't make assumptions without supporting evidence. However, where evidence points to game management on a driven grouse moor – and where farming and pigeon fancying interests have been ruled out – there may still be six or seven possible suspects, even without the list being extended to suspects on contiguous estates. This makes for an exceptionally difficult investigation. Considering the investigation of the whole range of crimes, from reset to rape, minor assault to murder, on the scale of difficulty to convict, raptor persecution is near the top.

The manner of death of poisoned victims is horrendous. Birds are sometimes found in incredibly contorted positions through death by poisoning. A Perthshire raven that was picked up had gone right back over on its tail and a white-tailed eagle in Angus had its legs stretched forward, talons clenched tight and its head arched back. Birds poisoned by carbamate-based pesticides suffer muscle contractions, which must be painful in the extreme.

Gamekeepers seldom give information about other game-keepers, and never in a manner that can be used as evidence; only as intelligence. In addition, they are usually far too defensive about public allegations that their peers are killing birds of prey, lending tacit support for illegal activity rather than condemnation.

In one sense gamekeepers may benefit from a neighbour killing birds of prey but this must be offset by the incredibly bad press that befalls all gamekeepers when birds of prey are poisoned, shot or trapped. And this is often just on the *assumption* that a gamekeeper had been responsible.

As will be seen from the criminal activity described in the following pages, convictions in relation to driven grouse moors are almost non-existent and, for various reasons, wildlife law in relation to these vast tracts of uplands in Scotland and the north of England is almost unenforceable. This situation needs to change. It's completely unacceptable to have an industry which is either above the law or can easily circumvent the law. It's almost 20 years since the author heard the then First Minister Donald Dewar, at the RSPB Bird Fair at Loch Leven, state that raptor persecution was a 'national disgrace'.

Though there have been some improvements in the game shooting industry the situation, at least on intensively managed grouse moors, remains as Donald Dewar described it. The Scottish Government needs urgently to bring this to an end and the Westminster Government needs to follow suit.

RSPB Scotland Raptor Persecution Report

DECEMBER 2015 – RSPB Scotland published their report on raptor persecution for the period 1994 to 2014, which gives us a clear insight into the extent of raptor persecution on driven grouse moors. With 779 confirmed incidents of raptor persecution during that period it makes depressing reading. In addition, there were 114 incidents where raptor nests were suspected to have been interfered with, 11 of these against golden eagles, 49 against peregrines and 50 against hen harriers. The same locations crop up time and time again, and are consistent with the estates most regularly investigated by the police. Since most of the incidents are discovered by accident we would need to be extremely trusting to think that the figure of 779 confirmed incidents was the true total. It is much more likely that, on at least one of the estates *on its own*, there were 779 raptors killed during the 20-year period.

In one of the most worrying incidents a satellite-tagged golden eagle was found dead in lower Deeside in May 2012. GPS recordings on 29 April 2012 indicate that this eagle was stationary in one area of Glen Esk in Angus for fifteen hours, from 6am to 9pm.

On 5 May 2012 it was found dead around ten miles away near Aboyne in Aberdeenshire with severe leg injuries. The post mortem examination of the bird concluded it most likely had been caught in a spring trap, breaking both its legs. The tracking indicated that it had then been moved, overnight, and dumped *still alive* under a tree at the side of a country road, where it died four days later. As well as the cruelty aspect, if the injured bird had indeed been dumped, the person dumping it was attempting to create suspicion on other totally innocent people.

The size of a golden eagle's talons raises some doubts about the spring trap theory. It would be difficult to fit one foot from an eagle into most traps, though of course two traps may have been set together. With both feet severely damaged they would have been useless and the bird would have been less dangerous to handle. Might it just have been released from the trap or traps and left to fly off to certain death by starvation. GPS tracking indicated the eagle moved from Glenesk to Aboyne *during the night*, which might put paid to this theory, though Dave Walker, author of *The Fieldworker's Guide to the Golden Eagle,* confirms that golden eagles sometimes do fly in darkness. Investigating this crime, the police searched an area of Millden Estate, the driven grouse moor in Glenesk on which Alma, another satellite-tagged golden eagle was found poisoned in 2009.

It is an outrage that during the 20-year period 27 golden eagles have been confirmed as poisoned, five as shot, one trapped and four nesting attempts confirmed as destroyed. Satellite tracking has made the recovery of eagle victims easier, but also shows that some of the birds have vanished without trace, sometimes in areas where there is a history of persecution. Also of concern is that during the period no less than 14 dogs had been poisoned. There was another in Perthshire that would have been included in these statistics had the shepherd not been close by and warned the dog off a poisoned grouse bait just in time. It is a wonder that an innocent person has not yet been killed by these lethal baits or even by handling their victims.

There is less information on the persecution of hen harriers in the report. Such evidence is more difficult to obtain since it is known that when harriers are killed steps are taken to remove any evidence that they were ever there, such as removing the nest and gathering up feathers if a bird is shot. Hen harrier numbers are falling rapidly. Covert filming and the increasing number of hen harrier chicks being satellite-tagged should begin to give a clearer picture of why this is.

Methods outwith the present law of dealing with these criminals – and please don't consider that those involved are anything other than criminals even though they may not have a police record – are urgently required and at long last one is currently being explored by the Scottish Government. In May 2014 Paul Wheelhouse, then the Minister for Environment and Climate Change, committed to the need for a comparative review of licensing and game bird legislation in other European countries. This was carried out and on 24 February 2017 the report, *A Review of Game Bird Law and Licensing in Selected European Countries*, was published.

Law-abiding shoot operators should have nothing to fear if licensing of shooting (or of some types of shooting) in Scotland is adopted – apart of course from the inconvenience that will have been foisted upon them by the criminal landowners, sporting agents and gamekeepers who persist in flouting the law.

Though in the years towards the end of the RSPB report there are less criminals amongst the landowning classes and their gamekeepers than at the start of the 20-year comparison period, the stats shown by RSPB in the last two years of this report, 2013 and 2014, remain a concern, with ten confirmed bird of prey persecution incidents in 2013 and eight in 2014.

General Licence Restrictions

General licences, issued by the statutory conservation agencies in the constituent countries of the UK allow, without personal application for a licence, an owner or occupier of land or someone authorised by that person, to kill or take wild birds specified within that licence. Limits on these general licences are that the birds must be killed or taken only for the reasons stipulated and subject to a list of conditions. Examples are a gamekeeper live-trapping a carrion crow to conserve other wild birds or a farmer shooting woodpigeons to protect growing crops. In simple terms the licences allow actions that would otherwise break the law.

OCTOBER 2014 – From this date Scottish Natural Heritage has had the power to restrict the use of general licences where they have good reason to believe that crimes against wild birds have taken place. Not only may this withdrawal of the use of a general licence be made against an individual, but can be made in relation to an area of land. Since most crimes committed against wild birds remain undetected, it follows that the most likely sanctions will be in relation to areas of land.

Naturally the sanctions by SNH cannot be just on a whim; they must have evidence on the balance of probabilities. This is the level of civil, rather than criminal, proof, and the evidence can be passed from the police to SNH through an information-sharing protocol. If this sanction is triggered by a single incident it is much more likely to be against an individual who has been witnessed committing a relevant crime. If against a piece of land, such as a farm or estate, it is likely to be a recent incident backed by some degree of history of similar incidents, none of which can be pinned down to an individual but showing a clear course of criminal conduct.

The fact that withdrawal of general licences has been made retrospective to the beginning of 2014 shows that the Scottish Government and SNH are well aware of the groundswell of opinion on raptor persecution and appreciate how difficult it is to achieve a detection, far less a conviction, for these crimes. A few quick-time results might now begin to turn the tide. There is no shortage of estates to pick from since the start of 2014. Even though 2015 seems to have been the date decided by SNH to begin to withdraw the use of the general licence there are still estates at risk.

While the removal of the right to control some 'pest' species is a good start, it is only part of the answer; there are certain estates to which the withdrawal of legitimate means of controlling corvids will be a minor hiccup. Nevertheless if they do not fall into line then they can't argue if a new tranche of sanctions is imposed.

Two Scottish Driven Grouse Moors Lose the Right to Use General Licences – or Have They?

NOVEMBER 2015 – Robbie Kernahan of Scottish Natural Heritage Licensing was interviewed on the BBC Scotland *Out of Doors* programme. The subject was the restriction of the use of General Licences on the lands of two estates in Scotland. These are the first restrictions imposed by SNH and are unlikely to be the last. SNH's website shows the area covered by the restrictions, and their terms, as follows:

> In line with *Scottish Natural Heritage's (SNH) published General Licence restrictions: Framework for Implementing Restrictions* we hereby give notice that a restriction has been applied to the land outlined in red overleaf. This restriction prohibits the use of General Licences 01, 02 and 03 on that land between 13th November 2015 and 12th November 2018. Please note that this restriction does not imply responsibility for the commission of crimes by any individuals.

The SNH website did not identify the estates to which the restrictions apply but Robbie named them as Burnfoot Estate near Stirling and Raeshaw Estate near Peebles. It was hardly a surprise and many folks will have identified them in any case from the maps and from the many poisoned birds of prey known to have been found on each over the years. It is no surprise that both are driven grouse moors.

The combined list of birds in the three licences are: great black-backed gull, lesser black-backed gull, herring gull, carrion crow, hooded crow, jackdaw, jay, rook, woodpigeon, collared dove, feral pigeon, ruddy duck, magpie, Canada goose. (From 2017 greylag geese resident in Scotland, as opposed to those that migrate here in winter, may also be killed under licence No 2). The revocation of the licence means that none of these birds may be killed by any means on the lands of the two estates.

So no one on these estates will now (legally) be able to utilise a multi-catch crow cage or a Larsen trap to reduce the crow population. No one there will (legally) be able to shoot a carrion crow or a woodpigeon if it comes within shotgun range, or will (legally) be able to put a shot through a carrion crow's nest to destroy the eggs. These seem less serious offences compared with shooting or poisoning a red kite or peregrine. If a criminal is audacious enough to carry out these serious breaches of the law will he be bothered by these new restrictions? This remains to be seen, though it is worth bearing in mind that the penalties available to the court for *all* of these offences are the same: a fine of up to £5000 and/or 6 month's imprisonment.

This is a good start by SNH. Might the next estate to have a restriction order be Glenogil or Millden in Angus, Glenlochy, Inverness-shire, North Glenbuchat, Aberdeenshire or Edradynate Estate in Perthshire? All of these have seen their share in recent years of recoveries of poisoned baits or shot or poisoned birds of prey, incidents that bring shame on game shooting.

Almost immediately these two estates appealed their revocation and the revocations were suspended. Not long after, in February 2016, the revocations were back in force. The SNH website had two notices stating

General Licence Restrictions Restriction 01/2015 (and 02/2015) DECISION NOTICE In line with *Scottish Natural Heritage's (SNH) published General Licence restrictions: Framework for*

Implementing Restrictions we hereby give notice that a restriction has been applied to the land outlined in red overleaf. This restriction prohibits the use of General Licences 01, 02 and 03 on that land between 13th November 2015 and 12th November 2018. Please note that this restriction does not infer responsibility for the commission of crimes on any individuals.

The announcement was comparatively low key. Why did SNH not blast this news from the rooftops, firstly as an embarrassment factor for the estates concerned and secondly to inform as many people as possible who may be taking access to these estates to keep an eye open and to inform the police if they suspect an infringement? The second surprise is that the reinstated revocation took effect from the original date, despite a couple of months having passed during the suspension when the estates could have been controlling what they would no doubt have referred to as 'vermin,' or at best 'pest species.' This was now only a penalty for two years and ten months rather than for three years.

The Term 'Vermin'

A brief digression here to discuss the term 'vermin'.

A letter appeared in *The Courier* in August 2016. The content of the letter related to types of Land Rover and the closing down of grouse moors but the part discussed here is the letter author's use of the term 'vermin'.

There is no control of vermin so the hill farmer's lambs are killed.

The grouse left will either die due to tic (sic) infestation or be killed by stoats and other vermin or some by raptors.

The term 'vermin' is used frequently. It is a vile designation, unless used for infestations of head lice, bed bugs or similar. It signifies a complete lack of appreciation and a true lack of knowledge of wildlife. The author of the letter didn't specify the 'vermin' that needed to be controlled to save farmers' lambs, though he might have been blaming foxes, badgers, white-tailed eagles and maybe even golden eagles, the larger gulls, crows and ravens. Giving him the benefit of the doubt that he only means foxes, which can legally be controlled, they are hardly vermin. Foxes might be pests to part of the community if they take lambs or ground nesting birds, but the same foxes take many rabbits, rats and mice. The control of these small mammals is beneficial to farmers. The fox is an amazing creature, having lived on its wits for centuries to avoid being exterminated by homo sapiens. It is a beautiful animal, most certainly not deserving the label 'vermin'.

We are off on the 'vermin' trail again in the second sentence. Stoats are referred to as vermin, and by inference probably other mustelids such as weasels and maybe even pine martens and polecats, all of which might take young grouse. All are fascinating animals with their own charm and beauty. All are much more beneficial than harmful to farming and forestry and probably only adversely affect poultry farming where there is insufficient protection for the hens or ducks, or game rearing.

Over the years – and indeed even yet – most species of raptor have been referred to by some gamekeepers as vermin. People who refer to birds of prey as vermin plainly have no respect for them and it would be hardly a surprise if they killed them when any opportunity arose.

Court Action on Licence Revocation

Returning to the licence revocations, this was good news, and at the very least would be an inconvenience to the estates concerned, both of which have been suspected of involvement in a variety of crimes against wildlife over many years. Whether revocations will be much more than an inconvenience only time will tell. In the meantime police officers would be unable to search the estates concerned unless there is reasonable suspicion that an offence is taking place or has taken place – all the more reason for the revocation of the licences being well-known to the public.

To assist in the policing of the revocation it would be hugely beneficial if a general power of entry and search of the land subject to the revocation be granted to the police concomitant to its duration. This would be welcomed by wildlife crime officers, who are all well aware of the estates in Scotland (and in England for that matter) where wildlife crimes, particularly towards birds of prey, are discovered with disgraceful regularity. This needs to be seriously considered by SNH and the Scottish Government. With the failure of current legislation making a difference on driven grouse moors the screws need tightened on the estates that overtly flout the law.

7 FEBRUARY 2016 – According to the *Sunday Herald*, Raeshaw and Burnfoot estates are taking SNH to court in relation to their grounds for revoking the general licences that hitherto allowed them to control certain bird species on their lands. This extreme arrogance is not unexpected coming from certain landowners and sporting agents. Perhaps the revocations have been more than an inconvenience.

For at least the last decade evidence of wildlife crime in the form of illegal traps and snares, poisoned baits and victims of poisoning have been found with disgraceful regularity on the same few estates in Scotland. The notoriety of these estates is not only well known to the police, to SNH and to the RSPB but also to other landowners and gamekeepers who are trying to keep within the law. Why do they not stand up and be counted instead of offering up weak and unconvincing excuses?

As the Scottish Environment Secretary said, we have in Scotland the strongest wildlife legislation in the UK. While that is certainly the case, some landowners try (and succeed) to circumvent it. Surely this indicates it needs to be made even stronger. If that means the licensing of shooting (or the banning of driven grouse shooting as many people want) then so be it. The voting public are losing patience fast.

The embarrassing aspect of the estates taking SNH to court is that they have been issued individual licences by SNH to carry out certain 'pest species' controls, though there is no elaboration on which species or by which methods. It is deplorable that the rich can often run rings round the law.

12/13 JANUARY 2017 – The judicial review in relation to Raeshaw Estate was heard by Lord Armstrong at the Court of Session, Edinburgh. The fact that general licences were revoked in respect of the two estates was by then well-covered by the media, in particular by one of the best investigative journalists on wildlife matters in Scotland, Rob Edwards of the *Sunday Herald*. In his article Rob confirmed the judicial review was prepared by David McKie of Levy and McRae solicitors, Glasgow. This firm represents most gamekeepers and landowners in Scotland (and also many police officers). David is quoted in the article as saying,

> Responsible game management practices are at the heart of what Raeshaw and its employees do. My clients are disappointed by this ruling.

Considering the extensive list of illegal activities discovered on this estate this claim is surprising, though lawyers generally work with what they are told by their client. If an estate is carrying out 'responsible game management' why would walkers on the estate regularly complain they are circled and spied on by the numerous gamekeepers? It is also of real interest that the estate is owned by an offshore company registered in Jersey, which would create difficulties in tracing the owner should vicarious liability become relevant. It is also interesting that the sporting manager is Mark Osborne, who has a similar function on many other estates in

Scotland and the north of England where raptor-related crime is also found with regularity. These include two I mentioned earlier: Glenogil and Glenlochy. He may, of course, just be unfortunate in that bad luck follows him around.

Where an estate has its right to use a general licence withdrawn, and that estate is under the control of a sporting agent who also controls other estates in Scotland, the likelihood is that the pest control regime is replicated throughout these estates. It would make sense that the withdrawal of the general licence was extended to also cover these estates.

27 JULY 2017 – In a revealing blog Mark Avery states that he was told by Mark Osborne that he (Osborne) is 'a very rich and powerful man'. His blog continues,

> I was told recently by someone involved in shooting that the sardonic remark going around the shooting industry is that 'It won't be Mark Avery who ends driven grouse shooting, it will be Mark Osborne' which indicates the low regard with which Mr Osborne is held by some of the people who, to his face, treat him as if he were their best friend.

This was the author's response to Mark's post:

> I agree entirely with the comment in your blog that Mark Osborne has done more than anyone else to lead to the real threat of the demise of driven grouse shooting. I just can't understand why he wasn't kicked out of having anything to do with grouse shooting years ago. Him being 'rich and powerful', along with the greed of some grouse moor owners, has no doubt had a bearing on this. When he falls from grace I hope he lands heavily.

It was really disappointing in the *Sunday Herald* article to read that a spokesman for Scottish Land and Estates (SLE), which represents landowners, expressed 'concerns' about the quality of the evidence in relation to the revocations. If this is the case then this is an exceedingly feeble position to take. SLE, as part of the Executive Group of Scottish PAW, the PAW Scotland Raptor Group and from frequent discussions with wildlife crime officers, are well aware of the estates and the individuals that are involved in raptor persecution in Scotland. They need to put their collective heads above the parapet and not come out with mealy-mouthed excuses like this.

28 MARCH 2017 – The written judgement has just been published and it is absolutely fabulous news that Raeshaw Estate has lost the judicial review.

The petitioner in the case was Lord Davidson of Glen Clova who, it was stated in the judgement, represented the owner of '*land near Heriot, Midlothian, which comprises a substantial rural estate of some 8,000 acres, much of which is grouse moor*'. The owner is not so easily established, given on the web as Raeshaw Holdings, Channel Islands. These are the difficulties the police encounter in trying to establish vicarious liability, though the shooting is run by William Powell Sporting, Banbury, Oxfordshire. An internet search on JM Osborne & Co, Banbury, Oxfordshire, shows that Mark Osborne is the managing director of William Powell. A good starting point if a prosecution for vicarious liability is required?

The evidence for the withdrawal of the use of general licences was based primarily on four set spring traps found during a police search on 8 May 2014 and which surrounded a small homemade cage which contained a live pigeon as bait to lure in birds of prey. Additionally, there were skeletal remains of birds of prey found nearby. These were near a crow cage registered to Raeshaw Estate and which, during the spring and probably up till the month of May, would no doubt be operated daily by the Raeshaw gamekeepers. Isn't it strange that they never saw the dead birds of prey and reported to the police that some furtive person had come

Deer killed by poachers' dogs (photo courtesy of Lancashire Constabulary).

A snared fox. Snares that could suspend or partially suspend a victim are illegal in Scotland.

A badger latrine near a sett can be a sign of 'current use'.

A polished badger run between sett entrances can be a sign of 'current use'.

Captive fox filmed at South Herefordshire Hunt Kennels (photo courtesy of HIT).

Member of South Herefordshire Hunt staff with fox cub (photo courtesy of HIT).

Poisoning with carbamate-based pesticides causes severe muscle contractions and a painful death. On poisoned white-tailed eagle 'White G' note clenched talons and head thrown back.

One of the poisoned red kites discovered near Conon Bridge on the Black Isle (photo courtesy of RSPB Scotland). Note the head thrown back in similar fashion to the white-tailed eagle.

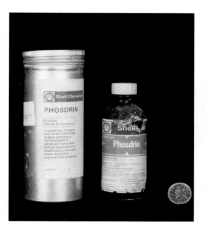

Mevinphos under trade name Phosdrin. One of the most deadly liquid insecticides used in wildlife poisoning (photo courtesy of SASA).

Tub of alpha-chloralose. Much of this white powder used to poison wildlife originated in Ireland (photo courtesy of SASA).

Pole trap discovered on farmland in East Devon (photo courtesy of Devon & Cornwall Police).

The River Lyon, Perthshire, with silt pouring in from mini hydro dam under construction (photo courtesy of SEPA).

The silt on the river bed suffocating freshwater pearl mussels.

A Larsen mate or clam trap. For corvid trapping when set with bait. This home-made version had springs so strong that would have made it illegal to use.

A pod trap. Also for corvid trapping when set with bait.

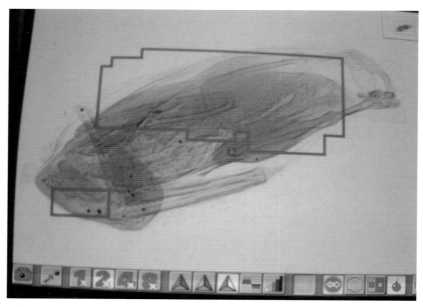

Cormorant x-rayed with prison x-ray equipment. X-ray clearly shows the shot in the bird and the photo was used in court.

A grouse moor with strips of burnt heather.

The pigeon in the cage on Raeshaw Estate surrounded by 4 set traps before the moss covering was removed from the traps.

And now the traps are clearly seen (photos courtesy of RSPB Scotland).

A multi-catch corvid trap with hooded crow as decoy. General licence conditions need to be met to use this trap. In Scotland the right to control 'pest' species can be withdrawn by SNH.

The satellite-tagged golden eagle 'Fearnan' found poisoned on the boundary of estates in the Angus Glens in December 2013 (photo courtesy of RSPB Scotland).

Male hen harrier bringing food to the nest (photo courtesy of Laurie Campbell).

Hen harriers normally nest in heather, making the eggs or chicks easy for a person to destroy.

Female hen harrier is often protective of its nest, making it easily shot.

Pole trap set and baited with pheasant on Brewlands Estate, Angus (photo courtesy of RSPB Scotland).

Grit tray for grouse. These only need occasional visits to top them up.

Poisons cache found by RSPB on East Arkengarthdale Estate (photo courtesy of Howard Jones, RSPB).

RSPB staff photographing one of the three pole traps found on Mossdale Estate (photo courtesy of Guy Shorrock, RSPB).

One of the three pole traps set on Mossdale Estate. Note down feathers on right hand spring, probably from earlier victim. (photo courtesy of Guy Shorrock, RSPB).

An unrestricted trap on a log over a ditch can easily catch a cat, pine marten or even an otter.

Buzzard caught in trap at Beinn Bhreac (photo courtesy of Police Scotland).

Masked gamekeeper attempting to release badger by shooting the snare off! (photo courtesy of HIT).

This badger ran off with a broken snare round its waist.
Death was almost inevitable.

on to the estate and either killed them or dumped them.

During a further police search one of the estate gamekeepers was found to have homemade traps identical to that in which the pigeon was being held captive. This was tremendous evidence and must have brought the situation close to the point where someone could have been charged with setting the pigeon cage and spring traps. All that may have been lacking was a wee bit of forensic evidence or an admission, though suspect gamekeepers invariably give a 'no comment' interview.

Historically, the written judgement mentioned that several poisoned buzzards (17) and a red kite, plus poisoned baits, had been found on the estate and, as seems often to be the case with the combination of satellite-tagged birds and driven grouse moors, a tag fitted to a hen harrier stopped working over Raeshaw Estate in 2011. There were many more criminal incidents discovered on the estate that were not mentioned in the report: a crow trap baited with two live pigeons, carbofuran, six shot buzzards, a poisoned raven, plus five dead barn owls, a tawny owl and a kestrel.

It appears that the estate staff had training '*in relation to the relevant legislation, and in relation to the possibility of prosecution, a corresponding disciplinary procedure which included the possibility of summary dismissal, and protocols and requirements in relation to the relevant reporting of the use of traps and pesticides and the maintenance of records*'. This was clearly ineffective, as was the investigation carried out by the estate, which concluded that '*nothing was revealed suggesting that any estate employee was involved in, or aware of, the (trapping) incident*'.

With this catalogue of criminality, of which many of the hill walking and conservation-minded public in Scotland had knowledge, it was strange that the Raeshaw Estate mystery owner remained blissfully unaware, otherwise he would have sacked all the keepers on the spot. Wouldn't he? He must wish now that he had, as the report claimed that '*the petitioner had been adversely affected by the consequential inference of criminality, and the associated actions of pressure groups*'.

Many people associated with grouse moors have been getting away with criminality for far too long. Thankfully, at long last, one of the battles on behalf of the public has been won. SNH can now review and make decisions on the backlog of estates at risk of having their general licence withdrawn now that the judicial review that stalled this process is out of the way.

SEPTEMBER 2017 – As a result of two poisoned buzzards being found on a Perthshire estate, Edradynate near Aberfeldy, details of the incident had been reported by Police Scotland to Scottish Natural Heritage. In September 2017, after an enforced delay awaiting the outcome of the Raeshaw appeal, SNH removed the right of the use of general licences on lands of Edradynate Estate. Following Raeshaw's example, the estate intends to appeal.

Slaughtering Mountain Hares to Increase Grouse Numbers

10 NOVEMBER 2013 – Investigative journalist Rob Edwards wrote an article in the *Sunday Herald* entitled 'The scandal of landowners shooting thousands of mountain hares every year'. There are several parts of Tayside where there used to be a great population of mountain hares, but now there are very few to be seen. They have been snared and shot to keep down tick numbers and to prevent louping ill, which adversely affects grouse. While mountain hares certainly carry ticks – as do sheep and deer – it is totally wrong to try to eliminate or even seriously reduce a species simply to allow higher numbers of another species: grouse.

On one driven grouse moor in the county of Angus not just mountain hares but deer as well were almost wiped out in the interest of grouse management. Worse, the deer were left where they were shot with no effort made to bring them into the food chain. Evidence was even obtained of a roe doe on a neighbour's land being shot from this rogue estate and left lying in the field. Not long after that a shooting tenant encountering a vehicle with unidentified keepers, a spotlight and terriers from that estate on land where they had no permission and apparently looking for badgers, and a neighbouring farmer found fox snares on his side of the boundary with several of his trees and bushes cut down to make a channel to guide foxes into the snares.

In relation to this illegal snaring incident, Tayside Police, with assistance from RSPB Scotland Investigations and using their equipment, set up covert surveillance. The snares had been knocked over first so that (1) they wouldn't catch any animal and (2) they would have to be re-set by the person involved. Twice they were re-set but frustratingly the wind moving grass and bushes had triggered the motion-sensitive camera so often that the battery had gone flat before the culprit could be caught on camera. Legal difficulties with covert surveillance are discussed later but in this case the difference was that it was being carried out on land where the owner had given permission, thus the police were able to obtain the level of authority required under the Regulation of Investigatory Powers (Scotland) Act 2000 [RIP(S)A].

People who were (or became) aware of some of these practices including gamekeepers, thought it an outrage, but knowing about these activities and finding evidence to bring anyone before a court are hardly the same. The annihilation of the hares was legal – though hardly moral – but the deer were being illegally shot at night using a spotlight and some of them out of season as well. The gamekeepers really were a bad crew.

On another driven grouse moor, in Perthshire this time, a neighbouring gamekeeper who strongly disapproved of the practice alerted the police to the fact that the gamekeeper was snaring mountain hares. The witness was even more disgusted when he saw some of the snares were set on the march fence. This gamekeeper had no objection to his neighbouring keeper reducing a white hare population by shooting but suspected the dead hares would be going into a hole somewhere. Even being used for dog food would be better but it is simply not right to see mountain hares killed and not either eaten or sold for food.

There is no argument that grouse shooting contributes to the Scottish economy and helps to keep some folks in a job, but striving for a monoculture of grouse on an upland estate, where any creature is removed if it in any way threatens grouse numbers is doing incredible harm not just to wildlife ecology but also to the shooting industry.

Grouse shooting, of course, is not the only use – and maybe not even the best use – that could be made of the uplands.

Are Mountain Hares Really Thriving?

MARCH 2015 – Two years on and there was an interesting article in *The Courier*. It was headed, 'Mountain Hares Thriving'. This may be the case in some areas of Scotland, but the article paints a rosy picture of mountain hares in the Angus Glens, where there are reported to be large numbers 'linked to last year's best in a generation grouse season'.

Unbelievably the spokesperson for the article was the headkeeper on Glenogil Estate, a driven grouse moor with one of the worst records in Scotland over the past decade for the recovery of poisoned baits and victims. Over 40 poisoned baits have been found on Glenogil Estate, with poisoned victims found including two white-tailed eagles and numerous buzzards. A further white-tailed eagle was reportedly shot on the estate, and several illegally-set snares and traps have been recovered, including a snare on a fence that held an injured badger.

The author has had the displeasure of being on Glenogil estate many times and has seen many more dead mountain hares in stink pits and as baits in or near various traps than were seen live. A quote at the end of the article on behalf of the Scottish Moorland Group states, 'Hare numbers are likely to go down where moorland is unmanaged or afforested but increase where managed for red grouse'. That may be the theory but this 'increase' seems incongruous with the purge on the tick.

Many people will be far from convinced by the article, and their doubts will not be assuaged by the choice of spokesperson.

Rewildling – and Subsidies

4 JANUARY 2017 – In his blog, George Monbiot, freelance journalist and co-founder of *Rewilding Britain*, shared his submission to the House of Commons Environmental Audit Committee inquiry, *The Future of the Natural Environment after the EU Referendum*. It is an incredibly enlightening article, but at the same time depressing and infuriating.

In summary, he declares that the hills of the UK are bare, which he says is down to the grazing of sheep and deer plus heather burning for grouse shooting. We have much less forest cover than other European countries, we have no large predators, such as wolves and lynx, and in any case there would be few places on moor and hill land for them to take refuge. He states that there are even more species to be seen on intensively farmed agricultural land than on much of the UK's moorland since a monoculture of heather suits relatively few species.

He defines rewilding as 'the mass restoration of ecosystems and the re-establishment of missing species,' and goes on to say that this 'could produce ecosystems here that are as profuse and captivating as those that people now travel halfway around the world to see. It has the potential to make magnificent wildlife accessible to everyone.' Monbiot takes Wales as an example and quotes that farming contributes just over £400 million to the economy, despite the subsidies it receives. Walking produces just over £500 million while wildlife-based activity generates £1,900 million.

It is likely that the differences in Scotland would be even more pronounced than in Wales so it may be that we need to switch away from the current use of the uplands, generate much more mixed woodland, broaden the range of wildlife on the hills and concentrate on industries like wildlife tourism. When using subsidies for land-based businesses it makes much more sense for a large proportion of the public to gain advantage rather than the current system where deer stalking and grouse shooting benefit only a few. These changes of land use may not suit all wildlife of course; golden eagles might move out of some present moorland ranges but at least there would be less likelihood of them being shot, trapped or poisoned.

The unfairness of subsidies is neatly captured in Monbiot's sentence, 'Farm subsidies are highly regressive, drawing money from the pockets of all taxpayers and delivering it to some of the richest people not only in Britain but in the world'.

Golden Eagle: Another Poisoning Scandal

DECEMBER 2013 – The poisoning of a satellite-tagged golden eagle, found dead on a driven grouse moor in the Angus Glens, is yet another reprehensible crime against our wildlife committed in that area of Scotland. This young eagle, named Fearnan, was ringed as a chick in a nest near Loch Tay in Perthshire in June 2011 and had spent much of its life in Badenoch, before it made the mistake of moving to the Angus glens in early November 2013. Three weeks later it had been poisoned.

It was the latest in a litany of raptor persecution incidents blighting Scotland's reputation as a place to come to see wild birds of prey, particularly the larger species such as the golden eagle and white-tailed eagle. The number of poisoned birds of prey, the number of poisoned baits, the number of illegally-set traps designed or baited to catch birds of prey and the traces of pesticide found in gamekeepers' vehicles, all in the Angus Glens, make it impossible for driven grouse-shooting estates there to argue that the responsibility for the death of this beautiful bird did not lie in their midst. Birds of prey are being sacrificed in order that the estates can produce the biggest possible grouse bags on a shooting day. This is a situation that is neither acceptable nor sustainable. We are at the stage where further government sanctions against grouse moor owners are desperately needed.

On one Angus driven grouse moor, Millden, there have even been trees – alder, birch and mountain ash – cut down by the sides of burns running through the moor so that birds of prey would have nowhere to roost. Some of the grouse moors are virtual deserts with little else except heather and grouse.

A clear culture has been emerging on some estates of poisoned baits being set round the boundary. Any victim is then equally likely (or *more* likely depending on the contour of the land) to be found on a neighbouring estate. This may have been the case with the golden eagle Fearnan and was exactly the case in 2008 when over 30 baits were found placed on the posts of the inner section of a double electrified deer fence on Glenogil Estate, while two victims, a white-tailed eagle and a buzzard, were found a short distance away, typically downhill from the baits, on a neighbour's land who had no shooting interests. Indeed the dead white-tailed eagle was found by and reported to the police by the distressed neighbouring landowner.

These situations make it incredibly difficult for the police to reach a successful conclusion in their investigation. Even if one of, say eight, gamekeepers on an estate set out the poisoned bait that killed a bird of prey that has been found, evidence needs to show beyond reasonable doubt that the bird of prey took bait set out by that particular person. In the absence of any bait found (or indeed even if a bait *is* found) this is an exceptionally difficult task.

Police wildlife crime officers, who are some of the most experienced and dedicated police officers in Scotland, need as much support from the public as they can get. This includes gamekeepers and other estate workers standing up and being counted. The main difficulty is that when a potential witness or informant is in leased accommodation or employed by a suspect, he or she will naturally be very reluctant to rock the boat. An estate shepherd one time was an excellent witness, whose evidence would most probably have convicted the estate gamekeeper of setting out a poisoned bait for a peregrine and of poisoning a golden eagle. While giving his evidence in court he went back on his original statement and the fiscal had no option but to desert the case. Some weeks after the abandoned trial the shepherd was made redundant and lost his tied house.

At the time of the recovery of Fearnan the Scottish Gamekeepers' Association said in their statement to the press

> The SGA will not condone the poisoning of birds of prey. If any SGA member is convicted of such a crime, they are removed from our organisation.

Even by October 2017 this remains their standard quote.

This is a feeble message to send out. There is no argument that the committee and many members of the SGA do not condone the poisoning of birds of prey. It has brought game shooting to the most unpopular state it has ever faced in the eyes of the public and is now courting sanctions that may result in considerable restrictions.

But the organisation must be well aware that the chance of any of their members being *convicted* is slight. They have been well aware over the years of at least one gamekeeper who regularly poisoned birds of prey yet took no formal action against him. Being a member of a representative organisation is not like being an employee, with the various employment rights afforded. Any of their members could be expelled at any time yet the SGA has allowed gamekeepers who they know are ruining the reputation of the organisation and its majority of decent members to continue their affiliation.

Gamekeepers and their organisations would do well to take whatever steps necessary to address criminality within their ranks. This is even more urgent in view of part of the Scottish Government commitment published in their annual Wildlife Crime Report at the end of 2016, which stated:

> We must protect the environment from those who seek to damage it for personal gain.

> We will increase the penalties for wildlife crime and consider the creation of new sentencing guidelines in line with recommendations from the Wildlife Crimes Penalties Review Group.

> In order to safeguard vulnerable species from illegal persecution, we will carry out a review of prevention measures including the operation of the Partnership against Wildlife Crime and supporting Police Scotland in their work to target wildlife crime hotspots. We are prepared to introduce legislation where necessary.

These threats by Scottish Government, which have been made several times over the preceding few years, seem to be real this time. The SGA has made a big fuss of the risk of its members losing their jobs if estates are licensed to carry out game management or shooting. Common sense dictates that the only risk will be to those members who continue with criminal activity towards protected wildlife. Surely the SGA or any other landowning, gamekeeping or shooting organisation would be better without them in their midst in any case.

'Vaporised' Golden Eagles

AUGUST 2016 – It was depressing news that yet another satellite-tagged golden eagle has disappeared in the Monadhliaths. In less than five years eight satellite-tagged golden eagles have disappeared, all in this grouse moor area. Satellite tags have proved to be very reliable and the chance of them all suddenly failing after working perfectly normally is a coincidence that even the most naïve amongst us would not accept.

The latest bird, named Brodie, was two years old and vanished in July 2016. The normal procedure with a satellite tag that has stopped working would be for the RSPB to discuss the disappearance with Police Scotland and get the green light to attempt to find the bird somewhere near its last known location. In this case there may have been no ground search; more likely a search from roads in the area to attempt to track a signal. Until that search is concluded the fact that the bird is missing in a particular area is unlikely to be made public.

Some gamekeepers maintain that golden eagles are not a problem, but eight golden eagles known to be missing in an area of grouse moors, together with a further golden eagle found poisoned in the same area in 2010 tend to confirm that golden eagles are still being eliminated.

I was pleased to see that Roseanna Cunningham, Cabinet Secretary for Environment, Climate Change and Land Reform, has ordered a review, stating,

I have instructed officials to analyse the evidence from around 90 surviving and missing satellite-tagged eagles, to discover if there is a pattern of suspicious activity.

Grouse moor management does help species such as curlew and golden plover as well as generating much needed rural employment and income but this cannot be at any price.

The public rightly expects all businesses in Scotland to obey the law. Let me be clear: grouse shooting is no exception.

As previously stated, the Scottish Government is prepared to introduce further regulation of shooting businesses if necessary. It will be unfortunate if the activities of a few bring further regulation on the whole sector, but that is the risk those who defy the law and defy public opinion are running.

The review cannot have any other outcome but to indicate highly suspicious activity. Hopefully it will be concluded in double-quick time before the list of poisoned, shot, trapped and vaporised golden eagles grows ever longer.

Hen Harriers

The hen harrier is one of the most beautiful and the most persecuted of all the raptors in the UK. They nest on the ground, normally in rank heather, and are hated on grouse moors as they take a number of grouse chicks, especially when feeding their own chicks. Having said that their main food is small mammals, especially voles, and small moorland passerines such as meadow pipits.

The 2016 survey of hen harriers showed that there was a 13% drop in numbers in UK and the Isle of Man from 633 territorial pairs at the 2010 survey to 545 territorial pairs in 2016. All of the constituent countries of the UK showed a fall in numbers with England, 67%; Scotland, 9%; Wales, 39%; and Northern Ireland, 22%.

For Scotland, the 'stronghold' of hen harriers currently with 460 pairs, this is the second successive decline revealed by national surveys. Over the last 12 years in Scotland the number of breeding pairs has dropped by 27%. England is in a far worse situation. In 2017, with the potential for at least 300 breeding pairs, there were only three successful nests from a total of seven attempts, with 10 young fledged. Four of the nests were on land managed by Forestry Commission.

The Shot Hen Harrier

DECEMBER 2012 – A first-class report by Bob Elliot, head of investigations at RSPB, on the BBC Scotland *Out of Doors* radio programme, which explained how far forensic science has advanced in relation to wildlife crime. The example being discussed was that of a female hen harrier found dead on 5 July 2012 on Thorney Grain moor in Colsterdale in the Yorkshire Dales, an area of driven grouse moors. The bird had a fractured leg and it was suspected it had been shot. Police officers have had many birds and animals x-rayed and the evidence of shooting is usually easily seen in the form of shotgun pellets still in the body or very small fragments of lead left in the body after a bullet has passed through or even if a shotgun pellet has disintegrated. In this case there were no such obvious signs.

Still working on the likelihood of shooting as the bird's cause of death, the Zoological Society of London (ZSL), where the bird had been sent by North Yorkshire Police for a post mortem examination, concluded that the bird was likely to have bled to death due to its injury, and in any case would have been unable to hunt, condemning it to death by starvation. The ZSL then passed the bird to the University College of London Institute of Orthopaedics and Musculoskeletal Science, Stanmore, where some pioneering forensic work was carried out. The scientists were able to photograph a cross-section of the leg bone and analyse one of the fragments. Foreign bodies in the bone fragment were shown to be of a radio-density consistent with metal, probably from a metal projectile. By fixing the bone fragment in a block of resin, and grinding and polishing the block down layer by layer, one of the particles was reached. The particle had entered the leg bone, had been deformed by impact, and was primarily composed of lead. The inevitable conclusion was that the bird had been shot.

Such advances in forensic work relating to wildlife, as shown here and also at Science and Advice for Scottish Agriculture (SASA) in Edinburgh are huge steps forward. We are also exceptionally lucky in Scotland in that work carried out by the SASA forensic science department is done free of charge for the police. But the difficulties for the police remain in obtaining evidence beyond reasonable doubt in wildlife cases, with identification of the person responsible being the most challenging hurdle, no more so than in the killing of birds of prey. Theories, assumptions and guesses do not constitute evidence.

The hen harrier in this case was found on a grouse moor. Gamekeepers on grouse moors are blamed for the decline in hen harrier numbers, and science (as well as crime intelligence and the covert filming of harriers being shot) tends to confirm this is the case. However a bird with a damaged leg could potentially still fly some distance and may not have been shot on the estate on which it was found. Years ago the author recovered a dead red kite in Perthshire that had its lower mandible shot off. This may well have happened near where the bird was found, or could in fact have happened many miles away.

Looking in more general terms at dead and injured birds of prey found on grouse moors, the person responsible *may* have been one of seven or eight keepers on the estates. The ideal situation is for a suspect to be interviewed 'cold,' in other words without any warning that might create an opportunity for the disposal of evidence or the concoction of an alibi. It is an organisational nightmare for the police to interview that number of suspects simultaneously, especially as they may be out at work and scattered over many thousands of acres. Search warrants may assist the investigation, but these legal documents are not handed out willy-nilly: there must be current intelligence or evidence that gives reasonable grounds to suspect that the particular person or people have involvement in the crime. This, of course, is not always available.

Even in interview, the gamekeepers from some grouse moors very often claim (if indeed they say anything more than 'no comment'), that they do not have their own 'beats' and that they all just muck in. Naturally this makes it much more difficult to link a crime to an individual. A press release has little chance of gaining evidence; it's not as if there are likely to be many witnesses out on the hill apart from sheep and (maybe) deer. It is a completely different situation compared to a press release asking for witnesses to a mugging in a city street to come forward. In any case for the police to release details of the finding of a dead or injured bird of prey before they have a chance either to obtain search warrants or interview suspects gives an early warning to the very suspects that it is essential for the police to take by surprise. A press release, however, should be made at the earliest stage; if nothing else it puts yet another wildlife crime in the public domain, but nothing is as simple as some of those who criticise from the sidelines make out.

On the issue of beats, on the larger estates gamekeepers invariably have responsibility for their own beat. Knowing whose beat a particular crime, such as an illegally-set trap, is on makes a police investigation slightly easier. Since a suspect is not obliged to say anything when questioned by a police officer it would be a helpful condition of licensing, should that be introduced, that the responsibilities of keepers for particular areas are mapped as a condition of a licence being granted.

Changes are required in the way legislation protecting raptors is enforced, especially so far as driven grouse moors are concerned. The police across Scotland have around 100 wildlife crime officers, some full-time and some with many years of experience of dealing with wildlife crime. They are often assisted by the National Wildlife Crime Unit or various statutory and charitable organisations, particularly in regard to bird of prey crime. Within the Wildlife and Environmental Crime Unit (WECU) there are now four very experienced prosecutors dealing with all cases of wildlife crime, environmental crime and animal cruelty and rapidly building up formidable experience. They are supported by a specialist member of Crown Counsel who provides support and legal advice on specific points of law or appeals in wildlife and environmental crime. There is also a communications officer from Crown Office and Procurator Fiscal Service (COPFS) Media Relations. Yet this array of strength is not working.

Conservationists, especially those involved in the monitoring of birds of prey, and the landowners and gamekeepers not involved in this intolerable and inexcusable slaughter (which excluding driven grouse moors, is quite a reasonable proportion despite some protests to the contrary) need to realise they are in fact on the same side. They need to report suspicious incidents, at the time and to the police. They also need to report any suspicions that certain individuals are involved to the police, to the National Wildlife Crime Unit or anonymously via Crimestoppers. This information is assessed and goes into the melting pot of intelligence, held on the Scottish Intelligence Database and available to every police officer in Scotland. Their piece of information may just be the crucial factor in enabling a sheriff to sign a search warrant.

Crimes Against Hen Harriers – Penalties

JULY 2014 – There were two very interesting interviews on the *Birders against Wildlife Crime* website, one by Mark Avery and the other by Chris Packham. Both were in relation to crime committed against birds of prey, focussing particularly on the hen harrier. The interviews were given on the back of an e-petition initiated by Mark which called for a ban on driven grouse shooting.

This was the first of three e-petitions by Mark to ban driven grouse shooting. This e-petition gathered over 22,000 signatures, the second, in 2015, nearly 34,000 and of course the third and by far the most successful, in 2016, over 123,000. This ably demonstrates the value of awareness-raising. If the public disapprove of an issue enough they will take action against it, in this case vote to have it banned. If they don't know about it how can they be expected to help with change?

Listening to the interviews, it was particularly revealing that neither are against shooting *per se* and indeed acknowledge that there are some benefits in grouse shooting. Their gripe – and that of a large proportion of the population of the UK who are aware of the issue – is that hen harriers are being killed to allow an increased production of wild grouse for shooting. Further, it cannot be disputed that the problem is at its most extreme on driven grouse moors. Driven grouse shooting is described by Mark as 'the worst example of a field sport in the UK'.

While there may indeed be some other causes that result in localised hen harrier declines, one would need to be foolish in the extreme to argue that hen harriers are not being killed by gamekeepers. Chris does not blame all gamekeepers or all estates and the common-sense points he makes is that the actions of some tarnish the reputation of the remainder. He is of the view that increasing penalties for those convicted of wildlife crime is not the answer.

Currently in the UK, under the Wildlife and Countryside Act 1981, a person convicted of an offence under that Act can be sentenced to fine of up to £5,000 and/or six month's imprisonment. In most cases this is quite a realistic penalty taking into consideration the range of other crimes carrying the same penalty. The exception may be if a company, a landowner or a person in a supervisory capacity is convicted or when the crime has been committed for commercial reasons. Having said that, a penalty of even £40,000 (as is recommended by the Wildlife Crime Penalties Review Group in Scotland) would be quite easily paid by many landowners and sporting agents. They may be more worried, however, of the proposed increase to 12 month's imprisonment on summary conviction proposed by the same group. The group's proposal of a term of imprisonment for up to 5 years on conviction on indictment should worry them even more.

A substantial penalty is no deterrent if there is minimal risk of being caught. Two examples spring to mind, one quoted by Chris in his interview. He quotes the £27k reward for information leading to the conviction of the person or persons involved in the recent killing of a large number of red kites and buzzards on the Black Isle. The reward still stands and no one has come forward with evidence that would convict. The availability of a penalty of even ten year's imprisonment in this case would therefore mean nothing. Conversely, when in 2000 (2003 in Scotland) courts could use imprisonment against wild bird egg thieves, Operation Easter, initially a Tayside Police and now a National Wildlife Crime Unit UK-wide operation, was already in existence. All UK police forces and RSPB were working together to pool and utilise intelligence and *the risk of detection and conviction was real.* That was the critical difference and there has since been a rapid decline in wild bird egg theft.

Crimes Against Hen Harriers – Sanctions

Before moving on from penalties, it needs to be understood that a sheriff or magistrate in a court cannot automatically issue the maximum available sentence. Much as we would sometimes relish this, a convicted person must be sentenced according to the severity of the crime, his means to pay, any early plea of guilty and any analogous previous convictions. Additionally, any mitigating circumstances would need to be considered. Imprisonment for a first wildlife offence would therefore be unlikely. The crime of a gamekeeper shooting a hen harrier, for instance, is not likely to be judged as serious as a landowner who orders this action, either directly or implicitly. We must also realise that a small number of sheriffs or magistrates, used to dealing on a daily basis with crimes relating to drugs, violence and dishonesty, may not necessarily see crimes against wildlife as top of their list of priorities in public protection.

There is no easy answer. Different solutions have been tried and have failed; in fact had hen harrier persecution ceased there would be no need for Mark's e-petition. Sadly intelligence shows that there is no obvious end in sight. The action to counter hen harrier persecution needs to be multi-faceted and include education, crime reduction, appropriate legislation, effective investigation and prosecution plus hard-hitting sanctions for those who are determined not to change their criminal conduct. A comment from Chris that we need to 'increase awareness and to motivate people to care' is so relevant. This means raising the issue at every available opportunity so that people who may sympathise with the hen harriers plight, *were they aware of it,* become aware. The hen harrier days that are now UK-wide should catch the eye of the media and garner public support for change. Most conservation organisations are well versed in good publicity so little more needs said on this aspect of attack apart from remembering not to isolate landowners and game managers who are already supportive.

Though vicarious liability is not the complete answer, it has had some crime reduction impact, though patently not showing an effect on all intensively managed driven grouse moors. At least it is another part of the armoury, but in Scotland only! Mark referred to 'crime in the hills... carried out in the early hours with no witnesses'. This activity is sometimes reported to the police as intelligence but to secure a conviction intelligence needs to be converted to corroborated evidence, which is extremely challenging. Nevertheless, if there is no intelligence flow to the police then they are unaware of particular illegal activity or who may be carrying out these acts.

While there is a well-trained and enthusiastic police wildlife crime officer network throughout the UK some of the officers get little support from the higher echelons of their force. Awareness-raising in respect of chief officers and (in England and Wales) police and crime commissioners would certainly pay dividends. These senior managers are not always aware of the strength of public feeling on raptor persecution – indeed on any wildlife or environmental crime – and in the past have been badly caught out by media coverage that sometimes exceeds that of a murder or rape. Even those officers who may be skilled in dealing with hare coursing and other wildlife crime but have not yet had to tackle raptor persecution can be guided and assisted during an investigation by the National Wildlife Crime Unit, in fact it would be prudent for all raptor persecution investigations to be run past the NWCU at the outset.

Obtaining evidence for a successful prosecution is fraught with difficulties. This is why alternative options may be the answer. Many estates are in receipt of huge subsidies, sometimes for keeping sheep whose main purpose may be in mopping up ticks that are killed off when the sheep are periodically dipped. Experience in the past reveals that infractions from one year could not be continued into the next year so that evidence of a series of wildlife crimes, enough to have subsidies suspended or reclaimed, was more difficult to establish. As opposed to (and in addition to) vicarious liability, which is a criminal procedure, the government reclaiming subsidies and suspending further payments needs to be considered as a real disincentive to commit crime and if this sanction can be altered to be used more effectively it may begin to make a difference. Some restrictions on clawing back subsidies have been put in place by the EU. So far there seem few advantages in leaving the EU but reinstating the earlier conditions under which subsidies can be reclaimed might be a good start.

JULY 2014 – There was a further interview on the *Birders against Wildlife Crime* website, yet again on the subject of bird of prey persecution, in particular the hen harrier. This time Charlie Moores, one of the founder members of BAWC, interviewed Bob Elliot, head of investigations at RSPB and working from their headquarters in Bedfordshire. Bob worked regularly with wildlife crime officers in Scotland and all who have worked with him have great respect for his knowledge of birds, his knowledge of wildlife law and his diplomacy.

Bob acknowledges the difficulties in preventing and detecting the killing of hen harriers and other raptor species, and is well aware of how difficult it is for the police to get evidence to get a case to court, far less to get a conviction. He is angry that the killing of hen harriers continues and, like many police wildlife crime officers, knows who the main players are. Bob said, 'We need more of the good guys, particularly gamekeepers, to come forward and tell us what is going on.'

The really frustrating aspect is that the 'good guys' in game management outnumber the 'bad guys' yet seldom pass to the police (or to the RSPB) their knowledge or suspicion of raptor-related crime. Because of what these criminals are doing, a large part of society has turned against the game shooting industry. Several years ago a keeper admitted that he would not go into town wearing his tweeds for fear of intimidation. This is unfortunate as in many cases land managed for shooting can have benefits for other wildlife. The author carried out a year-long wildlife survey on a north Perthshire estate, not managed for grouse but for driven partridges, and logged 90 species of birds during that time, including hen harrier, buzzard, red kite, kestrel, peregrine, white-tailed eagle, sparrowhawk and even goshawk. Golden eagles and merlin were frequent visitors but never seemed to be present on the survey days. (*A Wealth of Wildlife*, Thirsty Books, 2014)

It is perplexing that the industry allows a handful of real criminals (and these are sporting agents and keepers, backed by some landowners, who are well known to other landowners and gamekeepers as having a policy of eliminating any bird or mammal species that is in any way a threat to large bags of grouse on intensively managed grouse moors) to continue to operate in this way with hardly a word said against them in public. It is even more baffling that there is sometimes denial by those associated with land management that gamekeepers and their managers are even responsible for killing hen harriers.

The nettle needs to be grasped by the game shooting industry and information passed to the police that will help bring crime linked to game management to an end. As far as gamekeepers and their bosses are concerned, it is their livelihoods that are at risk. Bob is optimistic that harriers will one day be seen in suitable habitat across the UK but the sanctions currently imposed by the government in Scotland are most certainly not working against the criminals referred to. There is no doubt that in time – at least in Scotland – tougher sanctions will be imposed, but the patience of many people is running out.

As far as the north of England is concerned, there seems to be absolutely nothing in place that would in any way reduce, far less prevent, the killing of hen harriers.

Yet Another Shot Hen Harrier

12 AUGUST EVERY YEAR – This is the beginning of the grouse shooting season, traditionally referred to as the 'Glorious Twelfth'. The date is now more commonly termed the 'Inglorious Twelfth' since there is nothing to be celebrated about the crime committed on driven grouse moors.

APRIL 2015 – The satellite-tagged hen harrier 'Annie' originating from the Langholm Project was found shot. The bird went missing in March 2015 and the body was recovered on a grouse moor in South Lanarkshire six weeks later during a search by RSPB investigations staff after reportedly liaising with Police Scotland.

This scenario is not uncommon in relation to birds of prey, particularly the much-persecuted hen harrier. Disappointing in this case is the length of time taken before an announcement, in the first week in August 2015, that the bird had been killed. It is likely that the carcass, when found, was in a desiccated state, thus making the cause of death more difficult to establish. The author has been involved in many such investigations and the first action would have been to have it x-rayed. If the bird had been shot a cause of death would be established within hours. When a carcass is found in a really rotted or desiccated state it is often worthwhile to take half an inch of soil from immediately under the carcass and have it x-rayed as well in case any shot has seeped from the disintegrating body into the soil. For the same reason this is worthwhile with rotted or desiccated carcasses suspected to have been poisoned.

It is most unusual for a person committing an illegal act such as shooting a protected species not to dispose of the evidence. This makes it probable that the shooting of the harrier had not proved immediately fatal. Birds or mammals that are shot can sometimes live with pellets in the body depending on whether or not they strike a vital organ. Certain injuries might mean that the bird will die within an hour, 24 hours or even a matter of days. If this was the case here the bird could have been recovered a considerable distance from where the crime took place, and of course would not be able to be retrieved and disposed of by the perpetrator. It then makes the investigation extremely difficult for the police to solve, especially an investigation beginning three or four months after the commission of the crime and where it is unlikely that there was a witness to the shooting; at least a witness that was not in some way complicit.

It was disappointing to see on television that the news item majored on an interview with RSPB and not, as the statutory investigating authority, Police Scotland. In bird crime cases reporters often seek out RSPB rather than the police investigating officer but more effort needs to be made by the police to change this position. An RSPB comment or interview can always be used to complement the news item. The police are rightly non-political and unbiased, or at least should be. What has happened, with RSPB having taken the lead, is that everyone and their granny now thinks that they held back this news until just before the opening of the grouse shooting season.

Five Missing Hen Harriers

JUNE 2015 – In the north of England, five male hen harriers with females on nests mysteriously disappeared. The nests, in Lancashire and Cumbria, were all on land managed for conservation, but males provisioning a female on a nest may hunt some distance from the nest, including the crossing of estate boundaries. All were partners of nesting females, resulting in the nests failing.

During many criminal investigations police officers usually know the real story, and very often even the identity of the person committing a crime. Providing proof beyond reasonable doubt, however, is a completely different matter. It is unlikely that the police wildlife crime officers investigating these indents in Lancashire and Cumbria will find out what happened to the birds but they will certainly not believe that all have died of natural causes. The hen harrier is the most persecuted raptor in the UK and very few have chicks that fledge successfully on driven grouse moors. In persecution incidents generally the female harrier is shot off the nest but this is not quite so easy on someone else's land, unless it is done by a 'trespasser' after dark or in the early hours. Shooting, trapping or poisoning the provisioning male of the pair (or trio, as sometimes male hen harriers have two mates) means that the female has to leave the nest to find food. This usually results in the chilling or predation of eggs or chicks and the subsequent desertion of the nest.

One, or even two, males disappearing may be suspected to be as a result of natural causes but all or most of these five birds were undoubtedly the subject of persecution. The unfortunate issue is that there are no bodies that can be examined therefore any suspects or their apologists can argue that no crime has been established. From the policing point of view, the investigating officers can only work with facts and evidence, making the chance of solving the disappearance of these birds almost nil.

These may well have been most of the hen harrier nests in England that year and it is a disgrace that this beautiful bird has never been allowed to reach its breeding potential in England, where RSPB reckon there is sufficient habitat and food for at least 300 pairs. While it can't be proved that grouse shooting interests are behind the disappearance of these five magnificent birds, the fact they have all vanished simultaneously will strengthen the argument and the lobby against driven grouse shooting.

Alleged Disturbance of Prospecting/Nesting Raptors

DECEMBER 2015 – The blog *Raptor Politics* published an article claiming that there is an apparently legal strategy being used by estates in Lancashire's Forest of Bowland, an area of driven grouse moors, and elsewhere 'to deter raptors from returning to nest at traditional breeding territories, particularly at ground nesting sites'. The methods described in the article are strategically placing the following near traditional nesting sites:

- grit feeder trays filled with medicated grit used to treat worm infestations in red grouse
- tunnel traps deployed to kill 'vermin'
- using gas guns to frighten off hen harriers from moorland as they were displaying or prospecting for a nesting site

The allegation in relation to the first two methods is that gamekeepers are regularly visiting the grit trays and tunnel traps, and in so doing are disturbing the birds and making them move on before they start to nest. Whether or not these visits are being made with regularity, grit trays hardly need topped up daily, and there is no legal requirement to check tunnel traps daily provided they are set as per the Spring Traps Approval Orders. While that is the legal position, some conscientious keepers do like to check their tunnel traps on a daily basis.

There are some issues to consider before an offence is shown to be committed:

Is the bird at issue a bird listed under Schedule 1 Wildlife and Countryside Act 1981? The birds to which the article relates are most likely to be hen harriers or peregrines, both Schedule 1 birds.

If so, has it started to nest? In the case of a hen harrier, this would be as soon as it sets down the first heather twig on its chosen nesting place. In the case of a peregrine, which does not make a nest as such, this would be as soon as it begins to prepare its scrape. However very little in wildlife law is easily proved, none more so than proving the first steps of a nesting attempt. In Scotland, in relation to the hen harrier (but not the peregrine) it is protected under Schedule 1A of the WCA (birds that may not be intentionally or recklessly harassed at any time), as is the white-tailed eagle, golden eagle and red kite. 'Harassed', of course, is a slightly stronger term to that of 'disturbed'. Since we're talking about Lancashire this offence doesn't help.

Other than the Schedule 1A listed birds in Scotland, if the bird has *not* started to nest no offence has been committed. Regular disturbance of Schedule 1A birds could be construed as harassment, though of course Schedule 1A does not apply in England, the Westminster government having no interest in improving legislation that just might make life more difficult for landowners.

If the bird is included in Schedule 1 and has started to nest then it has to be proved that the action taken *did* disturb the bird and that it was carried out recklessly or intentionally.

To help in proving the last bullet point, whoever is aware of (or suspects) any of the strategies above should make contact with their wildlife crime officer at the earliest opportunity. If the Schedule 1 bird has indeed started to nest then the police officer can make contact with the gamekeeper(s) (and the landowner, bearing in mind *to knowingly cause or permit the offence, or in Scotland, vicarious liability)*, advise them of the bird's presence and the state of the nesting attempt, and that visits to grit boxes, traps or the use of gas guns could make them liable to being charged under the Wildlife and Countryside Act. If this is not done it is unlikely there can be evidence led that any offence was carried out recklessly or intentionally. (Don't have concerns about giving away the location of the nest to the keeper; a keeper is on the hill every day and, unless driving about with his eyes closed, will already be well aware of the location.)

In England and Wales, in relation to the much more limited use of the term 'recklessly' within the WCA, the absence of Schedules 1A and A1, and the absence of vicarious liability, this legislation urgently needs to be brought in line with the law as it is in Scotland. The Act should augment the term 'intentional' with the term 'reckless', and Schedules 1A (birds needing protection from harassment) and A1 (birds whose nest needs year-round protection) should be incorporated into the Act listing the relevant birds. This is an extremely difficult task with the present Westminster government but it is one of the first of several routes that could begin to address the problem.

Man With Gun and Harrier Decoy on National Trust Land in Derbyshire

APRIL 2016 – BBC news and other media featured a report by two birdwatchers of an alleged crime taking place on National Trust land in the Derbyshire Peak District, which ably demonstrates that a variety of different methods are utilised by criminals intent on getting rid of hen harriers. The birdwatchers had filmed a man who was hidden in heather, on National Trust land leased for grouse shooting, a short distance from a white plastic decoy bird. According to the witnesses the man had a gun and the dummy bird very much resembled a male hen harrier. Though the film is quite grainy, having been taken from half a mile away, the man and the decoy bird can clearly be seen, as can an item that looks very like a shotgun.

The incident, which took place in February, was reported to Derbyshire police, and it appears that their enquiries are complete and did not result in anyone being charged. Though this is extremely vexing it is hardly unforeseen as identification was always going to be problematic. Unless the police had some idea who the person was, interviewed him and obtained an admission, they would reach a dead end quite quickly.

But let's assume there had been identification, did an offence take place? Firstly, there are two independent witnesses able to speak to what they saw, this being backed up to some extent by what they filmed. The evidence of the two men would most likely be accepted by the court as they were two birdwatchers out to observe birds and stumbled across this incident. This is completely different from a person going on to land for the purpose of *looking* for offences being committed and, having found such evidence, capturing the evidence and reporting the matter to the police. It is this latter type of evidence that may not be accepted in court and this incident clearly shows the difference.

While it was suspected that the suspect's intention was to decoy then shoot a hen harrier this would have to be proved to a court beyond any reasonable doubt – not an easy matter. Though no hen harrier was seen, there is still a potential offence under the Wildlife and Countryside Act 1981, Section 18(2), which states:

> *Any person who for the purposes of committing an offence under the foregoing provisions of this Part (of the Act), has in his possession anything capable of being used for committing the offence shall be guilty of an offence and shall be punishable in a like manner as for the said offence.*

The 'said offence' in this case would be the shooting of a protected bird and the items 'capable' would be a shotgun and cartridges plus the dummy bird.

Proof of intent may depend on the witnesses that the prosecution and defence field for this purpose. The defence would contend that the decoy was to bring a bird that can be lawfully shot, such as a carrion crow, within shotgun range. There are much easier and less time-consuming ways of dealing with carrion crows but methods of dealing with hen harriers without leaving evidence of illegal activity are more difficult. It's doubtful that the prosecution would win this argument and it demonstrates the difficulty in obtaining convictions for wildlife crime linked to the protection of game, particularly on driven grouse moors where there may be several gamekeepers employed.

Pole Traps Set on Grouse Moor: Were the Targets Hen Harriers?

JUNE 2016 – Driven grouse moors were the subject of social media attention for all the wrong reasons. Firstly, it was claimed that a gas gun was being deployed on Broomhead Estate in the Peak District National Park. Broomhead Estate is a driven grouse moor, and the gun was placed just outside the boundary of, and pointing towards, a Special Protection Area (SPA). Its regular bangs would adversely affect any bird, nesting or otherwise, in close proximity.

This is not the first time that negative comment has been made about the use of gas guns on grouse moors. Until recently their use has always been on agricultural land to scare pigeon or rooks from crops. With the amount of bad publicity that driven grouse moors in particular continue to receive, one would think that any sensible owner, sporting agent or factor would instruct their employees not to carry out any activity that is likely to show the estate or grouse shooting in a bad light, whether or not the activity might be legitimate. By the continued use of gas guns on grouse moors it is plain that those responsible could not care less about public perceptions.

Hot on the heels of this story, a gamekeeper has been given a police caution for setting and resetting three pole traps on the Mossdale Estate, a driven grouse moor in North Yorkshire. A member of the public had found spring traps set on three posts at a remote corner of the moor. Particularly worrying was a hen harrier seen hunting nearby. He contacted RSPB Investigations, who immediately made their way to the area. The traps were made safe and covert cameras installed to monitor two of the traps. Sure enough, three days later, a young gamekeeper arrived to reset them.

When interviewed by the police the young keeper admitted the offences; he could hardly do otherwise since he was caught on camera. It is unacceptable that for such a serious crime as the use of pole traps to catch protected birds he only received a police caution. Aggravating the offence are the presence of the three posts on the estate, which seem to be there specifically for the purpose of pole-trapping, feathers on two of the traps, indicating that they had already caught victims, and the cruelty involved with this type of illegal instrument. There may be some element of the investigation to which we are not privy that justifies the mind-boggling decision of the police, but it is hard to imagine what it might be.

Demonstrating how far forensics relating to wildlife crime has advanced, the three traps were taken to Science and Advice for Scottish Agriculture (SASA) in Edinburgh for examination for blood and feathers. Evidence on one of the traps indicated that it had caught a kestrel while a second trap indicated that a falcon species, probably a merlin, had been caught.

There must be a lesson here for middle management in the police to be made much more aware of the seriousness of wildlife crime and the public revulsion at the level of raptor persecution. It would be surprising if the police officer dealing with the case did not realise its severity but was over-ruled and did not feel sufficiently confident to go to a level above whoever made the completely unprofessional decision to deal with this crime as a caution.

It is also worth thinking about the position of any estate owner or sporting agent who directs, encourages or countenances illegal activity in order to boost grouse numbers. Many driven grouse moors are owned by a mixture of lords, dukes, earls, knights and barons as well as bankers, businessmen and companies based in offshore tax havens. Grouse moor owners and sporting agents may think of themselves as respectable citizens but in fact some of them undoubtedly sit at the highest level of wildlife criminals, with their minions killing by proxy and carrying the main risk of prosecution. If a case could be proved against the owners and sporting agents there is little doubt that they would receive (and thoroughly deserve) a substantial jail term, and with a bit of luck would have to forfeit hundreds of thousands of pounds under Proceeds of Crime legislation for the value added to grouse shooting by illegal activity such as the killing of birds of prey.

As a consequence of the Mossdale Estate incidents the gamekeeper involved is no longer employed by the estate, though whether he resigned or was sacked is not known. Neither is it known if he is now working elsewhere as a gamekeeper.

The estate was formerly a member of the Moorland Association but has since resigned its membership. Did the owner jump or was he pushed?

After being deluged by letters of complaint, the following explanation and apology was written by temporary assistant chief constable Amanda Oliver:

North Yorkshire Police has now completed a review of this investigation. This involved looking again at the evidence and the decision, using the Ministry of Justice Guidelines on Adult Cautions, the Adult Gravity Factor Matrix, and the latest Director of Public Prosecutions Guidance on Charging. Specialist advice was also sought from the Crown Prosecution Service.

Our review found that we had not used the correct cautioning guidelines when dealing with this case. Police officers have a level of discretion in deciding how to deal with a case, based on the specific circumstances of the incident. However, the review concluded that if the correct guidelines had been used, it is likely that the man would have been charged, rather than cautioned.

It is important to remember that a police caution is not a 'let off'. A person who has been cautioned has a criminal record, and there can be very serious consequences as a result. Depending on the circumstances, they may lose their job and income, and there may also be implications for the person's future employment. A decision was also made to revoke this man's firearms licence as a result of his involvement in this offence.

As a result of the review, we asked the Crown Prosecution Service to consider whether further action should be taken on this case, and provided them with other details of our activity related to the man involved. After consideration, the Crown Prosecution Service decided that, taking all matters into account, including that a decision had already been made, no further action should be taken.

I would like to reassure you that the mistake we made on the use of guidelines was isolated to this particular case. Nonetheless, we have taken the matter very seriously, and we have ensured we have done everything we can to avoid mistakes happening in the future. We have amended our policy on how wildlife crimes are dealt with by investigators and decision-makers, and advice from specially-trained officers is now sought in every case. We are also using our position as the National Police Chiefs' Council lead on rural and wildlife crime, to share what we have learned with other police services across the UK.

Thank you for raising this matter with us. On behalf of North Yorkshire Police I would like to apologise for the distress that this matter has caused you, and assure you that we will do our very best to protect our local wildlife, and deliver the police national wildlife action plan here in North Yorkshire and more widely.

Yours sincerely
Amanda Oliver, Acting Assistant Chief Constable

Ms Oliver is known to have a genuine interest in her force dealing professionally with wildlife crime. It would be a good bet that she was furious at the way her force dealt – or more accurately failed to deal – with this incident.

Missing Hen Harriers and Abandoned Raptor Persecution Cases

JUNE 2016 – Bad news from RSPB: yet another hen harrier had disappeared. The bird was a female, satellite-tagged as a fledgling in Scotland in 2014, and her last known position was at the end of May 2016 on a grouse moor in South Lanarkshire. RSPB Investigations staff made a search of the area but there was no trace. This missing bird follows hard on the heels of four harriers satellite-tagged, also in 2014, in the Forest of Bowland by Steve Downing, and now also missing. (Steve was formerly the wildlife crime officer for West Yorkshire Police and is now heavily involved with the Northern England Raptor Forum). The most recent of these four birds to go missing was on 16 April 2017 in County Durham. Satellite tags can fail, though this is unusual, and an extraordinary coincidence if that occurred in all five cases. Harriers also die of natural causes or are taken by other predators, but in those cases the signal would continue and the body of the bird can normally be found. Death is therefore most likely to have been as a result of a particularly nasty unnatural cause, with the criminal quickly disposing of the evidence.

In addition to these incidents there have been others where harriers are known to have been shot. In June 2013, gamekeeper was charged with having shot a hen harrier on Cabrach Estate, a grouse moor in Morayshire. It took almost three years for charges to be brought. Video footage, obtained by a covert camera placed by the RSPB, was made available to the Crown. The case dragged on and a date was eventually set for an intermediate diet on 21 April 2017. The case was not called: it had been abandoned by the Crown.

An RSPB press release of 5 May 2017 stated:

Court proceedings against a former gamekeeper, accused of shooting a protected hen harrier, have been dropped by the Crown Office, who have indicated that after considering all of the relevant material they could not use RSPB Scotland video evidence to support the prosecution in court.

RSPB then made public the video footage taken. It showed a female hen harrier flying low into the frame, most likely having been flushed from a nest in the heather, and being shot. A man with a shotgun then passed through the frame and returned seconds later carrying what most certainly looked like a dead female hen harrier.

It is exasperating that this case was discontinued. A statement released by Crown Office following the RSPB press release gives the reason for dropping the case as the footage being obtained by RSPB entering the land, presumably without the consent of the landowner, for the purpose of gathering evidence for prosecution. It stands to reason that the landowner would not be contacted by RSPB for permission otherwise the chances are that no crime would have been carried out or – more likely – the perpetrator would have taken steps to ensure that he was either not filmed or was not identified.

There was an enormous tide of public disgust at the failure of the Crown to take anyone to court; in fact the furore at its non-result is probably unequalled in wildlife crime. The national press, BBC television and social media carried numerous accounts and all showed a mix of anger, frustration and claims of corruption at the Crown's failure to prosecute.

Police officers know better than most the rules under which COPFS must work. Some wildlife crime officers are also aware that in previous meetings between COPFS and RSPB the charity has been told that it is unlikely that evidence will be used if it is gained by covert surveillance carried out on what is termed 'private land'. Surveillance like this is deemed to be the remit of the police after having obtained relevant authority under the Regulation of Investigatory Powers (Scotland) Act 2000 (RIP(S)A). That does not make the very obvious commission of a crime by a presumably identified person any less acceptable. It is even more vexing when a gamekeeper covertly filmed shooting a hen harrier in Morayshire in almost identical circumstances in 2001 was convicted and fined £2000.

Two professors, Professor Duff and Professor Glover from the Law Department of Aberdeen University wrote articles on the failure of the Crown to take proceedings in the Cabrach Estate incident. Both agreed that as the law stands the Crown made the correct decision based on the stated case Lawrie v Muir 1950. This case created the guidance in Scots Law where evidence that has been obtained irregularly does not make that evidence inadmissible provided it has been obtained in good faith, though what has also to be taken into consideration, in Professor Duff's interpretation of Lawrie v Muir, are:

> the gravity of the crime; the extent of the irregularity; the urgency of the investigation; the need to preserve evidence; the authority and identity of those who obtained the evidence; the motive of those responsible for the impropriety; the extent of the infringement of the accused's rights; and the issue of fairness to the accused

If the trial judge makes a decision based on the above which is thought wrong and is appealed, again in Professor Duff's words:

> the appeal court will determine whether the trial judge got it right or wrong in legal terms, either in admitting the evidence or, very occasionally, in excluding it where there has been a prosecution appeal on a point of law.

It is a pity that this is not the route that was taken in the Cabrach incident. An appeal court may have agreed that there are unique circumstances in trying to obtain evidence of a crime against an endangered bird that takes place in a remote area, more especially so when the video footage only covered the immediate nest area where no one should have been in any case unless they were there for the purpose of breaking the law. It would have been interesting to see if an appeal court may have considered that the circumstances met sufficient of the criteria to allow the covert surveillance evidence. Could law and common sense have agreed?

If a crumb of comfort can be taken out of this incident it demonstrates even more strongly that raptor persecution continues and the urgent need for effective sanctions against driven grouse moors. It is to be hoped that Roseanna Cunningham, Cabinet Secretary for Environment, Climate Change and Land Reform, will consider this as yet another almost insurmountable hurdle in convicting wildlife criminals, especially on driven grouse moors. Driven grouse shooting would be better banned altogether, though if this incident and the absence of a satisfactory outcome helps licence driven grouse shooting then we may consider there has been some sort of a result.

There have probably been countless incidents of raptor persecution on Cabrach Estate going back years. The estate was the subject of many visits by PC Dave Mackinnon, who was the wildlife crime officer for Grampian Police in the 1990s. The catalogue of crimes found on the estate include 11 buzzards found stuffed into rabbit burrows after having been shot, the discovery of over 20 poisoned baits, pole traps set, including evidence of an inoffensive barn owl being trapped. Additionally, a gamekeeper was convicted after being found with a poisoned peregrine in his vehicle while another was convicted of shooting buzzards.

MAY 2017 – Digressing slightly from hen harriers but still on the theme of abandoned prosecutions, on 12 May RSPB Scotland released a second video recorded covertly by them which filmed a man setting a pole trap. The recording had been released as the Crown Office decided not to proceed with the case.

Briefly, the background is that in July 2015 RSPB Scotland staff discovered an illegally-set spring trap placed on top of a pheasant carcass which had been placed on a pole. This effectively made it a pole trap and was most likely to catch a bird of prey by the leg as it landed on the trap. The estate involved was Brewlands Estate in Glenisla in Angus, though the same criminal scenario may well be played out almost anywhere in the UK. As well as driven pheasant and partridge shooting Brewlands Estate offers walked-up grouse shooting.

The RSPB staff sprung the trap and deployed a video camera (which they happened to have with them?) covertly. They made contact with the police and a few days later attended with the police to recover the trap and check the camera.

The camera showed that the trap had twice been re-set and the police managed to identify the person setting it, who was charged with the offence. A report was submitted to the procurator fiscal but the case was eventually abandoned before proceeding to trial on 15 May 2017. Though no reason was given for discontinuing the case it seems likely that it was for the same reason as the first case: the use of covert surveillance on 'private' land without permission of the owner of the land.

When there is such clear evidence of a crime being committed it is exasperating that the perpetrator is not brought to justice. RSPB Scotland investigations staff are aware that their evidence might not be accepted for prosecution for the reason above so are they right to continue to use this method?

What were the alternatives for the RSPB?

They could have made contact with the police as soon as possible and reported the incident. The police then had various options to contemplate. They would have considered trying to obtain authority under RIP(S)A to deploy covert surveillance; even the use of the RSPB's equipment under police direction, but as the current law stands this authority is unlikely to have been granted. The offence, if charges were to be brought under the Wildlife and Countryside Act, would not have been deemed serious enough to permit RIP(S)A authority as the maximum penalty is only 6 months imprisonment.

The difficulty for the police is that they cannot go on to private land to undertake covert surveillance without RIP(S)A authority. This cannot be given except in cases of serious crime, defined as where the conduct is an offence for which a person who has attained the age of 21 and has no previous convictions could reasonably be expected to be sentenced to imprisonment for a term of three years or more, or involves the use of violence, results in substantial financial gain or is conduct by a large number of persons in pursuit of a common purpose.

'Substantial financial gain' can be made on a driven grouse moor by killing off raptors which in any way negatively affect the numbers of grouse on the estate that can be shown over the guns on a shooting day. Large sums of money are charged for a day in a grouse butt and because of the financial gain through criminality the police should be able to justify the use of covert surveillance of a nest at risk or a trap set for a bird of prey. Are these the circumstances in which the Lord Advocate encouraged the 'specialist prosecutors in the Wildlife and Environmental Crime Unit to work with Police Scotland to ensure that law enforcement utilises all investigative tools at their disposal in the fight against wildlife crime'? These may be the circumstances but where are the tools?

It is in these situations that the police could begin to address wildlife crime on 'private' land were the maximum penalty made more severe. In England and Wales the maximum penalty for animal cruelty offences is to be increased to five years from 2018. The Scottish Government is also of the view that animal cruelty penalties are insufficient and intend to address this. Surely the more serious wildlife offences equate to those under animal cruelty legislation. Increasing in parallel the maximum penalty under the Wildlife and Countryside Act, the Protection of Badgers Act and the Animal Health and Welfare (Scotland) Act would make sense, would be in line with the review by Professor Mark Poustie and would allow the police to apply under RIP(S)A legislation for authority to carry out covert surveillance.

The seriousness of the crime in the Cabrach and Brewlands cases discussed is massively under-represented and the facility to try on indictment and the ability to imprison for at least 3 years is essential at the next round of legislation change. COPFS would no doubt have welcomed that option if anyone had ever been reported for the Black Isle poisoned red kites and buzzard case.

Recovery of DNA at Brewlands might have been another option, but that cannot be guaranteed, especially when a trap had been exposed to the elements. There is also another possible method involving a contaminant, though this requires regular, probably daily, monitoring as the material can be quickly spread from the suspect to other people not involved.

None of these methods is straightforward and there is no doubt that the action the RSPB took was the most likely to obtain evidence, though at risk of being deemed inadmissible. Increasing political pressure may currently provide better dividends than trying to secure a prosecution given the difficulties in meeting evidential requirements.

So we return to the question of RSPB Scotland's dilemma and whether they took the correct action. They cannot be blamed for taking that route. They may have had reservations that a court case would follow but their action brings the crime to the attention of the public. Furthermore, any failure to prosecute adds to the argument for change in the law. It also demonstrates yet again that wildlife crime is still taking place on shooting estates, though it is logical that the level must be far in excess of the few that are discovered.

Police officers, particularly detective officers, are very aware through case law that the interests of an accused person must be balanced against the interests of the public. These last two cases show an exceptionally strong bias towards the accused. It seems as if there is a stalemate unless legislation or procedure can be altered to redress the balance.

It is to be hoped that if the two estates are in receipt of single farm payment they are ordered by Scottish Government Rural Payments Inspections Directorate to repay a year's worth of that payment.

Further, details of the crimes filmed should be passed by the police to Scottish Natural Heritage so that the privilege of the use of general licences on the land is withdrawn.

Will the landowner be prosecuted for vicarious liability? Bear in mind the wording of the legislation:

There is no requirement for the employee to be successfully prosecuted for the offence (of vicarious liability) though for a successful prosecution of an employer, manager or agent, the Crown will require to prove who committee the alleged offence and the connection between that person and the employer, manager or agent.

Returning to harriers, since only a fraction of harriers are fitted with satellite tags there must be many more harriers killed or nests destroyed where the deed is known only to the criminal involved.

Hen harriers are so regularly killed off that the police, conservationists and government must consider who has a motive to do such a thing. Of those working in the countryside farmers, shepherds and foresters have no gripe with harriers. Gamekeepers on low ground should have no problem with harriers, though unfortunately some still hate any bird with a hooked beak. The problem unquestionably lies with grouse moors, particularly driven grouse moors where grouse numbers are king and to hell with other wildlife that may be detrimental to grouse.

Hen Harriers – Good News and Bad News

It is heartening to report some good news in the form of Heads up for Harriers. This is a PAW Scotland-driven initiative to encourage estates to work with conservationists and have cameras put on harrier nests to monitor activity and identify some of the threats to the eggs and chicks.

2015 was reasonably successful, with 30 nests fledging in excess of 100 chicks in hen harrier Specially Protected Areas (SPAs). 2016 was less successful, probably due to the weather, with two nests on five of the estates involved failing for that reason and another losing one chick to fox predation. Twelve young fledged in total, but with any nesting species of bird, especially those that nest on the ground, there are always good years and bad years.

None of the results are surprising. Extreme weather and predation can affect hen harrier breeding success, just as they can in grouse breeding success. Both species have coped with these problems for hundreds of years. Grouse, of course, don't have to contend with their eggs or chicks being destroyed through human interference or the parent bird or birds being shot (at least at nesting time). The cameras, unfortunately, won't stop all of this, nevertheless it is a step in the right direction and full marks to participating estates. I wonder if any of the estates involved are Glenogil, Millden, Glenlochy, Raeshaw, North Glenbuchat, Leadhills, Burnfoot, Cabrach. I somehow doubt any of them will have any harriers there to nest.

One of these estates, Leadhills in Lanarkshire, has had the reputation as one of the worst estates in Scotland for raptor persecution. There has been no grouse shooting on the estate, possibly from about 2013 onwards and it is reported, though not confirmed, that in 2017 there were nine successful hen harrier nests. If that is true – and it's a big 'if', what does that say about the removal of hen harriers from driven grouse moors and their ability to bounce back once associated criminality ceases?

This good news of Heads up for Harriers is tempered by bad news. Between 2003 and 2006, during some of the worst years on the estate for raptor persecution, the shooting lease was held by Leadhills Sporting, of which Mark Osborne was listed as a director. The most extensive wildlife crime search ever conducted in Scotland took place on Leadhills in 2006, with the gamekeepers being detained and interviewed by the police. There were no charges but shortly after that Leadhills Sporting gave up the lease.

It seems that Mr Osborne is back in charge at Leadhills again as applications for licences to shoot ravens were made to Scottish Natural Heritage between 2015 and 2017. The applications were on notepaper headed JM Osborne & Co. The blatant shooting of a short-eared owl and a hen harrier on Leadhills in May 2017 shows that criminality has resumed.

APRIL 2016 – One of the 2014 satellite-tagged hen harrier chicks from the Forest of Bowland, named Highlander, was reported missing. The last signal had been in Country Durham. Many hen harrier chicks are now fitted with satellite tags. Some go missing and are found dead through natural causes since, even when dead, the signal should continue to operate allowing the body to be recovered. Far too high a proportion go missing in suspicious circumstances, with a hitherto perfect signal suddenly stopping.

JULY 2016 – A 2016 satellite-tagged harrier, given the name Elwood, disappeared on 27th July in the Monadhliaths. This is the area in which eight satellite-tagged golden eagles have also 'disappeared.' Professor Des Thompson, Scottish Natural Heritage, who is the Chair of PAW Scotland Heads up for Harriers group, said:

> The loss of Elwood is very worrying, particularly given the reported loss of eight satellite-tagged golden eagles in the same vicinity over the last five years. We are reviewing these incidents and will report our findings in due course.

May the findings be part of the report being prepared for Roseanna Cunningham?

SEPTEMBER 2016 – Another satellite-tagged hen harrier missing: this was a chick fledged that year in Perthshire and was given the name Brian. Its signal stopped abruptly on 22 August near to Kingussie, an area of driven grouse moors. Despite searches the bird was not traced.

OCTOBER 2016 – Satellite-tagged hen harrier 'Rowan' was found dead in Cumbria, with a clear shotgun wound to her leg. The same month a satellite-tagged hen harrier was seen at a roost near to where Highlander spent her two previous winters. Unfortunately the bird could not be identified since there was no signal from the satellite tag. The bird was confirmed as an adult female with no colour rings but having a BTO ring on the right leg, as did Highlander. The tag aerial was bent slightly to the left, as had been that of the missing Highlander.

In relation to the satellite tags they should last for up to 5 years and appear to have only a 4% to 6% failure rate. Highlander's tag had still been functioning earlier in her life despite the slight bend. The mystery may yet be solved, though by November 2017 there appear to have been no further sightings.

DECEMBER 2016 – 'Beater' went missing in the Scottish Borders and is presumed dead, as are two other harriers that went missing in the same month; 'Bonny', who went missing near Geltsdale and 'Mick' in the Yorkshire Dales.

JANUARY 2017 – Satellite-tagged harrier 'Carroll' was found dead in a farmer's field near Alnwick, Northumberland. Though this bird had died of natural causes, when x-rayed there were two shotgun pellets lodged in her body. The entry wounds had healed and being shot was not thought to have been a contributory factor in her death. Nevertheless it further demonstrates the extent of persecution of these glorious birds.

Other harriers that have disappeared without trace are 'Tarras', who disappeared in the Peak District National Park, and 'Donald', who disappeared in northern France. 'Hermoine', who died of natural causes on Mull was traced because of the signal from the tag. Because of the radio tags most or even all these birds should have been located – unless of course someone removed the tag. In October 2017 the 2016 tagged harriers still known to be alive are Aalin, DeeCee, Finn, Harriet, Sorrel and Wendy.

AUGUST 2017 – Two dozen hen harrier chicks were satellite-tagged by RSPB in 2017, mostly in Scotland. The first of these has already 'disappeared'. On 12 August, the opening day of the grouse shooting season, the last signal given by the hen harrier given the name Calluna, tagged on Mar Lodge Estate in July, was transmitted over a driven grouse moor on Deeside east of Mar Lodge and a few miles north of Ballater.

Allied to this missing harrier was a letter to The Times newspaper in early September 2017 by the director of communications for the Game and Wildlife Conservation Trust. In relation to an inference by RSPB (and indeed many others) that this bird had been killed on the grouse moor, he was critical of RSPB for claiming that GWCT 'ignored facts to suit its narrow agenda'.

The main point of including this is that the letter went on to say:

> The most productive location for hen harrier nests, 47 fledged young from 12 nests, was achieved by gamekeepers on Langholm Moor just three years ago. However, their improvement of the moorland habitat and protection of these ground nesting birds from foxes has now ended, because conservationists could not agree on how to also recover grouse numbers. Should hen harrier numbers drop to the two pairs there were before these gamekeepers arrived in 2008, the birds might ask who has the narrowest agenda.

Surely the reason for 12 successful nests, as part of the Langholm2 project, was because keepers had been ordered not to kill them. Other keepered moors having 12 successful nests must be rarer than hen's teeth, even with fox control.

We should bear in mind that the fate of these birds is only known because of satellite-tagging. How many untagged hen harriers disappear without trace? The persecution of hen harriers is the biggest disgrace committed against any wildlife species in the UK. We await the Scottish Government's resolution, with the latest information in September 2017 that the chair of the group leading the proposed review is about to be chosen.

The Westminster Government, under Conservative leadership, will do bugger all.

Poisons Cache Found on a Driven Grouse Moor in North Yorkshire

DECEMBER 2016 – Guy Shorrock is a senior investigations officer with RSPB, working from their headquarters at Sandy in Bedfordshire. In December 2016 Guy published an account of a cache of poisons uncovered on a driven grouse moor in North Yorkshire. Though the incident began in 2014 it was sub judice and details could not be released as they could jeopardise the outcome of any case.

In summary, RSPB Investigations staff had well-founded suspicions about illegal activities on East Arkengarthdale Estate, having been aware of a poisoned buzzard found there and Guy himself having seen an unidentified person with a Land Rover taking a pot shot at a sparrowhawk, albeit these incidents were slightly dated. Guy was also aware of a cage trap that had been – or was being – operated in a small plantation on the moor and he and a colleague decided to check it out since they are sometimes operated illegally.

It is interesting that on this evidence alone a police officer could not have carried out this check (or search as it would be determined) and expect any illegality found to be acceptable in court; it would be held to be a 'fishing expedition'. On the basis of the information given by Guy there would not be enough evidence for a search warrant and, if a police officer was relying on powers of search within the Wildlife and Countryside Act the incidents would have to be recent or there would need to be a clear seasonal course of illegal conduct. Police, as the statutory enforcers, must stick to these rules but NGO's don't have to, though at the end of the day prosecutors and courts would need to make a decision on whether to accept any evidence gained.

The principal objective of the RSPB with these searches is to uncover wildlife crime, especially that relating to raptors, but if no conviction follows at least incidents are brought into the public domain. It could be argued that these strict guidelines that limit search on private land may not be in the public interest and that they give landowners and their employees an unfair advantage. However there are several examples in case law where legislation has been seen to disadvantage the public and changes gradually made to balance the interests of the public against the interests of a suspect.

In December 2014 Guy and a colleague visited the cage trap, but found it was no longer in use. Shortly afterwards they found a buried bucket, discovered only because of a small piece of blue plastic that turned out to be part of the lid showing through the pine needles. Further investigation revealed that the bucket contained a small plastic tub which was part-full of a white powder. They discussed whether to mount surveillance on this bucket or to hand the case over to the police. The decision they made was to take a small sample of the powder for analysis and to return with surveillance equipment.

Was this the correct choice? From what Guy wrote there is no indication that they knew what the substance was at that point and only suspected that a crime was being committed. If they had *known* a crime was being committed it could be argued that they should have passed the case on to the police. RSPB have no official remit to investigate crime but are fantastic at assisting the police to do so; indeed they are better than many police officers in a raptor-related crime investigation.

Skipping ahead a bit, surveillance equipment was installed and in the few days since Guy and his colleague had first found the bucket it now contained an additional tub of powder, from which they again took a sample.

After several checks, on 16 March 2015, some three months

after the discovery, the RSPB surveillance showed a man removing the large plastic container, then replacing it later that day. Their check on the bucket showed that the small plastic tub was gone but there was now a sachet of a pesticide called Ficam W, the principle ingredient of which is known to be bendiocarb. Some ten weeks after the initial discovery the matter was reported to the police and a joint investigation made by North Yorkshire Police, Natural England and RSPB Investigations. The large container had held Cymag, the smaller container had held alpha-chloralose and the sachet, as the label indicated, had held bendiocarb.

The man filmed by the covert surveillance was believed to be the gamekeeper. He was interviewed by the police and made 'No comment' responses to questions. During a search he was found to have an electronic calling device with an interesting selection of the calls of raptors and predatory birds. This is illegal to use for the luring of birds to be caught or killed unless licensed.

The case was reported by the police to CPS but for a reason unspecified CPS did not take the case to court.

It is doubtful that this case would have been taken to court in Scotland either considering the circumstances. There was some good detective work here by RSPB Investigations but was it ever going to be admissible as evidence? A limiting factor for the police and for prosecutions is how far behind Scotland the legislation is in England and Wales. It was also obvious during the one-sided and clearly pre-determined debate resulting from Mark Avery's petition to ban driven grouse shooting that the Westminster government thinks everything is fine and has neither any intent to ban driven grouse shooting nor to improve wildlife legislation to make it any more effective.

This gamekeeper, by his own admission during an appeal against his firearms certificate being revoked (which he won and is another sad story) left deadly substances in the open and not under lock and key. Cymag, which has been banned since 2004, releases fast acting hydrogen cyanide when exposed to moisture. Unless a person has access to an antidote it can kill quickly. In addition he had bendiocarb, an acutely toxic carbamate-based insecticide, and the slightly less dangerous alpha-chloralose. In Scotland leaving these substances where they could be – and indeed were – accessed by the public could constitute culpable and reckless conduct. This may have given grounds for surveillance under the control of the police, which is always difficult on private land as has already been explained.

All three chemicals in this case, in Scotland, are included in the list of prescribed pesticides under the Possession of Pesticides (Scotland) Order 2005. The possession of these without valid excuse makes a person liable to a fine of up to £5000 and/or 6 months imprisonment. This is far easier to prove than under the Food and Environment Protection Act and the Control of Pesticides Regulations which police in England and Wales still use, or even an offence under the Wildlife and Countryside Act 1981 of being in possession of items capable of being used for committing an offence.

And then there is vicarious liability, which the Westminster government thinks is not required…

It is likely that the suspect's temporary removal of the Cymag on 16 March would be for gassing a fox den with cubs, or even a badger sett somewhere on the estate. In relation to his firearm certificate if he had been sacked, as he should have been, and shunned by other keepers and landowners, as he should be, he wouldn't have needed a firearm certificate.

A number of questions are posed by the investigation of this incident and need to be considered.

Sceptics may wonder why a corvid trap would be worth checking in the month of December, since almost all use of the varieties of these traps is made in spring and summer. The most common corvid trapping offence relates to traps not in use, therefore not being checked daily. These are sometimes left in a state in which birds can still enter but cannot escape. The trapped birds in these situations die of starvation. Apart from corvids there have been investigations with starved kestrels, buzzards, sparrowhawks and a golden eagle.

In relation to the cache it was surprising that Guy didn't identify Cymag at the outset because of its extremely unique fumes. Anyone who has encountered Cymag and caught a slight whiff of the fumes would know it again immediately. Because of the health and safety risks it is not a substance that can just be stored anywhere and must be taken to an agency with suitable storage facilities. It should certainly never be stored at a police station.

If the sample was submitted for testing on the day it was recovered, the result of the tests – even the field identification of the substance by an expert without the need to test – would have been available almost immediately. If that is the case then the incident would have been confirmed as a crime and should have been reported to the police at that point.

The man whose cache it was, and who was filmed by the surveillance equipment, was not clearly identifiable from the photo shown in Guys report. Nevertheless there was every chance that the clothing worn by the man could be recovered by the police during a search and the items could be compared with the clothing in the photo(s). The combination of clothing, together with the fact that the man was a gamekeeper on the estate and would have a motive and the ability to have such pesticides or insecticides, would go a long way towards proving a case. There may also have been fingerprint or DNA evidence available and also the chance to recover a similar bucket or tub under the suspect's control. Unfortunately there was nothing in Guy's report about the evidence from the police search.

From the facts given in Guy's report it is unlikely that police in England would have been able to obtain RIPA authority for surveillance on private land. There is no doubt this would be in Guy's mind too when he made the decision to deploy the RSPB surveillance.

Though the action that the police could have taken in Scotland has been described, there seems no equivalent of culpable and reckless conduct in England. Even without more knowledge of the circumstances and better understanding of police powers in England and Wales there would probably have been mileage in utilising a contaminant such as Smartwater, a similar product, Cyphermark, or even ultra-violet paste to contaminate any person handling the cache or contents. All these are detectable under ultra-violet light. The difficulty with this process is that (a) the items need checked regularly, even daily, to see if they have been handled and, (b) there needs to be a suspect that can be traced soon after any handling and preferably before he or she starts to spread traces of whichever product is used to others. This makes the result much less conclusive.

So, in the absence of any public explanation from CPS as to why they did not proceed with the case, the question must remain whether it was lack of identification from the photograph(s) or evidence which was compromised based on the action taken by RSPB. Despite some good work from a partner agency, in a situation like this legislation most certainly favours the criminal and disadvantages the public.

The Grief of Grouse?

DECEMBER 2015 – It was widely reported in the shooting community that a broad variety of bird species are thriving on some grouse moors. Surveys were carried out on three Tayside estates as part of *The Gift of Grouse,* a year-long campaign to 'highlight the wide range of benefits of grouse shooting and moorland management'. Grouse are lovely birds to look at and to listen to on moorland but it is questionable that they are a 'gift' to anyone but a select few. These surveys, if true since there has been little detail put in to the public domain, go some way – a very short way – to ameliorating negative publicity associated with grouse moors.

Of the three estates, many times in the past the author has walked over Glenogil Estate in Angus, an intensively managed driven grouse moor, to recover poisoned baits or their victims, or to seize illegally set traps and snares. On those visits the estate was like a desert, with little to be seen other than a monoculture of heather and grouse. Now 63 different bird species have apparently been noted, though the documentation of raptor species seen would have been interesting. The list of *nesting* raptors in spring time would be even more interesting, especially if chicks had fledged successfully. Changes *may* have come in with the arrival of the new owner, and if so these are to be applauded. Ultimately it is an estate owner who calls the shots, irrespective of the views of his employees, whether they be a sporting agent or head keeper. If, repeat, *if* there have been changes there may be more good news from Glenogil, but no one should hold their breath.

The second Angus Estate surveyed was Invermark, which has some driven grouse and considerable deer stalking. This estate is well known to the author, who assisted with several gamekeeper training courses there. It is not a surprise that the survey showed 81 bird species on the estate, specifically mentioning ten species of raptor. The estate was always extremely helpful, encouraged access, and the factor participated in a police-chaired project aimed at trying to reduce wildlife crime. The one niggling undetected crime on that estate is that the tree used by nesting white-tailed eagles, the first pair to nest in the east of Scotland for over 100 years, was cut down in January 2013.

The Perthshire estate was Glenturret. It has some driven grouse and is also trying to increase numbers of grey partridges. The estate was one of the first participants of Operation Countrywatch Partnership, a project which the author co-chaired and which was designed not just to reduce wildlife crime but to increase dialogue amongst disparate groups which should in effect have had similar aims. This estate boasted 61 species which from visits linked to Operation Countrywatch Partnership included most species of raptor. It was a delight to read that ring ouzels are thriving there.

So there is a modicum of good news here. Long may it continue.

Dead Red Kite and Destroyed Raptor Nests
Add to Moy's Disgraceful Reputation

JUNE 2016 – The Moy area of Scotland, just south of Inverness, is synonymous with raptor persecution, though the most recent conviction was in 2011 when a young gamekeeper, James Rolfe of Moy Estate was found in possession of a dead red kite. This was found in the back of his landrover when it was searched by police. Rolfe was fined £1,500.

According to a BBC news report in June 2016, wildlife crime officers from Police Scotland are now investigating yet more bird of prey persecution incidents. These relate to late May of that year, when four buzzard nests and a goshawk nest in the Moy Forest at Tomatin were found to be abandoned, with evidence at some of the sites of deliberate disturbance.

These incidents occurred on land where individuals from the agency responsible for the land were monitoring the nests. One of the first elements the police consider is motive. In this case, where the agency is Forestry Enterprise Scotland, there would be no motive to get rid of birds of prey since they do no harm to trees.

A practice has developed in some areas where illegal activity such as this stems from people responsible for neighbouring land, which must yet again point the finger of suspicion at game management. The Moy area consists mainly of driven grouse moors so gamekeepers on at least one of these moors must be considered by the police as possible suspects. They have the motive, ability and opportunity, whereas farmers are unlikely to have the motive and someone 'wandering in off the street' is unlikely to have any of these three elements. The missing – and crucial – element of course is identification.

Despite the efforts of dedicated and well-trained police wildlife crime officers, with all forensic aids at their disposal, it is unlikely that this series of crimes will be solved. The criminals may well be part and parcel of serious and organised crime, who (or at least their employers or supervisors) stand to gain large sums of money through increased grouse availability because of the illegal disposal of birds of prey. There is a reasonable clear-up rate with serious and organised crime, but adding wildlife into the equation completely changes the expectation, with the crimes taking place on what are effectively vast tracts of 'private' land and no doubt often under cover of darkness.

The owners of land used for forestry would have no reason to withhold permission from RSPB for covert filming, and in fact would almost certainly encourage it. In a future year this may be an option for RSPB to gain evidence for a successful prosecution.

North Yorkshire, the Worst County in England for Raptor Persecution

AUGUST 2016 – Raptor persecution continued in North Yorkshire, with an appeal for information by PC Rob Davies of the force's Rural Task Force after the remains of another buzzard which contained shotgun pellets had been found near Manfield. It was noteworthy to see that this bird had at least 11 shotgun pellets in its body, one in the head and three in the area of the lungs and heart. From the location of these pellets there is a good chance that the bird, if not killed instantly, would have fallen from the sky (or from wherever it was shot) at the point it was hit.

That would give the most likely location for the offence being committed as opposed to the bird being wounded and flying off to die elsewhere. This should help to limit the list of suspects. Often these can be found by using the force's shotgun registration system and postcodes relevant to the area.

It does pose the question, though, as to why the bird was not picked up by the person (the criminal) shooting it and disposed of.

This buzzard adds to the shocking North Yorkshire 2016 tally, published by Raptor Persecution UK, of 'several illegally spring-trapped buzzards, several shot buzzards and at least ten shot red kites'. This in addition to the report of the gamekeeper filmed setting three illegal pole traps, narrated earlier, on Mossdale Estate.

Traps

Several types of traps are used perfectly legally in the control of 'pest' species. For the control of certain birds that can be considered to be pests, particularly crows, large cage traps and the smaller Larsen traps are in the most regular use. Larsen mate (clam) traps and pod traps (see photos) are also used and in most cases all four of these traps are used legally, the most common offence being that of failing to check the trap and causing unnecessary suffering to either a decoy bird or to birds that have been caught. All of these traps, plus innovative home-made varieties, can equally be used illegally for the trapping of raptors by the simple use of a pigeon as a decoy.

In addition to the illegal use of the traps described, this part of the book will show a recent trend in the increase in the illegal use of mammal traps, especially Fenn-type traps, to catch raptors. This seems to counterbalance the slight reduction in the use of poisoned baits. These traps are shown to have been set on posts as pole traps, set on the ground near a bait that would tempt a bird of prey over the trap and catch it by the leg, or even set in this manner in conjunction with a Larsen or home-made design of trap with a pigeon as bait.

There are several examples of this illegal use in the incidents which follow.

A Cat Caught in a Tunnel Trap

OCTOBER 2016 – A report that points to other illegal activity taking place on driven grouse moors: on the *Raptor Politics* blog there was an account of a police investigation by Lancashire Constabulary into a cat that had been illegally trapped. The photograph on the blog showed a cat, still alive, hanging by the back leg from a Fenn trap which had been set on a log over a ditch or similar waterway. The estate is quoted as Bleasdale Estate in the Forest of Bowland, a well-known black hole for raptors. Bleasdale Estate is described in *The Field* magazine as being one of the 'best 50 sporting estates in the UK'. The estate includes a grouse moor of 6,000 acres.

In the *Raptor Politics* blog there were many serious accusations against the police officers involved. It would not be fair to comment on these accusations as there is no way of establishing their veracity, though they seem to relate to earlier complaints regarding damage to Fenn-type traps. Nevertheless it is worth giving a view of the use of the trap in which the cat was caught.

The trap is a Fenn type trap, probably a Mk IV rather than the larger Mk VI. It had been set on the log and covered by wire mesh, but had no restriction at either end to prevent non-target mammals entering or being caught.

For two reasons this trap has been set illegally.

(1) In England the Spring Traps Approval (England) Order 2012 governs the setting of traps for mammals. The trap needs to be *approved*, which is the case with the Fenn Mk IV, but it is only an approved trap if the conditions of approval are observed. In the case of this trap set on a log over a waterway the trap must be covered over, (generally by wire netting, though the covering is not prescribed) and the entrance at each end must prevent species larger than those listed in the Order as legitimate targets from gaining entry. The largest of the species listed is the grey squirrel.

Whoever set this trap, by failing to restrict the entrances, had therefore set an *unapproved* trap. In England, under section 8 of the Pests Act 1954, it is an offence to use or knowingly to permit the use of any spring trap, other than a trap that has been approved by Order, for animals or in circumstances for which it is not approved.

(2) Anything that flows from this illegal setting would also be an offence. Here we have a cat caught by a leg and left to suffer, according to a vet who examined it, for at least three days. This is

a further offence, this time under the Animal Welfare Act 2006, in which it is an offence to cause unnecessary suffering to any animal.

Contrary to what many people think there is nothing set out in legislation about the checking of traps such as the Fenn trap, which are meant to kill quickly *if set as approved and for the correct species*. If it is set outwith the approval conditions any animal injured as a consequence could come under the jurisdiction of animal welfare legislation.

An independent expert who examined the trap concluded that it would be highly likely that other traps and snares on the estate would be set in a similar illegal manner. This seems entirely logical. While part of the police investigation clearly focussed on damage being caused to traps and snares on this estate, which seems to have been ongoing since 2015, there is no clue as to what, if any, investigation they carried out in relation to this or any other illegally-set traps. Previous experience shows that where one trap is set illegally it is likely to be one of a series set in a similar fashion.

It seems reasonable to expect that if tunnel traps were being set illegally, this fact should have been picked up and investigated by the police much earlier, and certainly during any scene of crime examination of the alleged damaged traps in the 2015 investigation.

One of the biggest difficulties in the investigation of tunnel traps, whether on a log over a waterway or elsewhere, is that there is no maximum size set out in law for the entrance to the tunnel. Some of the trap users make no effort to restrict the entrance, some make a half-hearted effort by shoving a couple of sticks into the ground that a hedgehog could easily bulldoze out of the way, and some make a clear choice to stay within the law by making the entrance from either a piece of board with a hole drilled in it or a piece of gridweld mesh. There is no determination on the distance the trap must be from the entrance to prevent a curious or hungry animal being caught by the paw. There is no registration of the user of the trap as there is with snares and – to a degree – with corvid traps. Lastly there is no recognised code of conduct for the setting of tunnel traps.

These failings need to be addressed and a chance to do this is coming. Both DEFRA and the Scottish Government are working on changes to trap legislation. Under the Agreement on International Humane Trapping Standards (AIHTS) Fenn traps and some others are no longer considered humane for some fur-bearing mammals. In the UK this applies to stoats, even though they are not caught here for their fur. A new design of trap is required and tests are being carried out. This is an ideal chance to incorporate changes that will prevent, or at least minimise, by-catch.

Illegally-Set Trap on Aberdeenshire Grouse Moor

17 JANUARY 2017 – Walkers found a number of traps set on logs over burns where there was no restriction to the entry of mammals or birds not the legal targets. The location was on Glendye Estate in Aberdeenshire, another grouse moor. Photographs and details were published on an excellent blog written by one of the walkers, David Adam, but unfortunately there was no mention as to whether the police had been informed.

Between 17 and 20 January the incident had been reported by others on social media and it would not have taken long for the phones of the keepers on the estate to be red hot warning them of the widespread public knowledge of these crimes. If they had set the traps they would be there in a flash to remove them. The initial article stated that the walkers had left the traps in the set position, leaving them liable to catch a mammal or bird, so it was probable that they had informed the police. That was even more likely since the writer seemed a very responsible person who, like many of us, has a hatred of wildlife crime.

The bridge traps in question appeared from the photos to be Fenn Mk IV traps set either in wire mesh tunnels with no restrictions on the ends or simply with a single loop of fence wire over the trap. The single loop of wire method is much more unusual, though may have been placed there as a 'jump', in the manner of snares set for mountain hares, to encourage any larger mammal to jump over the trap. Either of the traps could easily catch protected species such as pine martens or even wildcats, and these larger mammals would be unlikely to be killed outright and more likely to be trapped by a leg and left dangling from the log, as was the cat described earlier.

The use of these traps in this illegal condition is pure laziness on behalf of the person setting them and it takes little effort to surround the trap with a proper wire cage. Gamekeepers state they are professionals and if a gamekeeper set these (and on any grouse moor regularly patrolled by gamekeepers it is hardly likely to have been anyone else) there is nothing professional about them.

Part of the Scottish Gamekeepers' Association quote on the incident is 'all traps operated must be set in accordance with the strict guidelines governing their use'. It's a wee bit more than 'guidelines' that govern their use, it's legislation. The criteria for setting these traps are not something that might be advisable to do, they're conditions that *must* be followed.

It transpires that the police had indeed been informed but when they visited the estate the day after the incident the traps had gone. The police learned that the walkers had informed the estate about the illegal traps and the gamekeeper had removed them. Another chance for someone to face justice missed, or did the witnesses take photographs to show the illegality? Reporting illegal activity to the police should be the first action to take. Telling anyone who could be a suspect about the discovery is just plain daft.

The Scandal of Spring Traps Set in the Open

JULY 2016 – An RSPB news release announced that Police Scotland was investigating another wildlife crime on a grouse moor. In fact it was on a driven grouse moor named as Invercauld by the chief executive officer of the Cairngorms National Park, within whose boundaries the estate lies. A common gull had been found with each of its legs caught in illegally set spring traps. A dead rabbit had been used as bait.

In summary, two hill walkers had found the gull struggling in the traps. The witnesses had told the estate about their find (Oh no, not again!) and also contacted the SSPCA because of the injured gull. SSPCA had attended initially and had euthanised the gull, and later Police Scotland, assisted by SSPCA and RSPB Investigations had carried out a search of the moorland area. Evidence was found that six other traps had been set with dead rabbits as bait but by then had been removed (which was to be expected since the estate had been alerted to the crime). This evidence would be in the form of small square indentations in the turf to accommodate the traps, a hole where the trap would have been pegged, and possibly some of the material (grass or moss) lying nearby that had been used to cover the traps. Some of the baits may also have been discarded nearby. There may also have been some evidence of a 'lead-in' to the trap, often in the form of branches or heather stems, directing the victim over the trap to get to the bait. If these various pointers were present then the police would have absolutely no doubt a trap had been set there.

It is unfortunate these other traps had disappeared as the police may well have gained DNA evidence leading to the criminal. This was a case where the police search should have been carried out the following day at the latest, though it was a few days before it took place. If this is the case this is where Police Scotland really need to get their act together and have a wildlife crime officer that can attend immediately, even if from another division.

This is a perfect example of where it would be advantageous to have the wildlife crime liaison officers in the different divisions working as a unit. It may, of course, have depended on when the police were informed of the incident by the SSPCA. Whatever the reason for the delay, unless the police search had been carried out right on the heels of the initial SSPCA visit to euthanise the gull there was no way they were ever going to recover the traps before they were removed by the estate. With their limited powers and the likelihood of encountering difficult individuals (as was the case when dealing with the snared deer and foxes on Glenogil Estate) it would be sensible for SSPCA to request to be accompanied by the police when attending to wildlife incidents on shooting estates.

Spring traps such as these, legal if set in a tunnel as described earlier, are more commonly abused than we realise. Until the point that they catch a victim they are extremely difficult to see. In this case, especially on a grouse moor, it is likely they had been set for some species of raptor, but of course they are completely indiscriminate.

In 2010, in the county of Angus, a number of spring traps set in the open were located round the perimeter of pheasant release pens. Several illegal snares were also set in the same area and in due course the gamekeeper was charged. He pled guilty to the snaring offences but denied responsibility for the traps, despite the fact they were round a pheasant pen which he was attending on a daily basis. He was one of the first people to be sentenced under the improved snaring legislation and was fined £200, the sheriff considering that the snaring offence was at the lower end of the scale.

Returning to the Invercauld Estate incident it has been widely condemned. Grant Moir, CEO of the Cairngorms National Park said,

> It is appalling that spring traps have been illegally set resulting in the death of a common gull. The law on the use of traps is clear and it is simply unacceptable for them to be used in this way. I have this morning asked for a meeting with the Head Trustee of Invercauld Estate and with the Sporting Partner to discuss these issues. I have also written to Police Scotland and other public sector partners to ask for a meeting to discuss resourcing further enforcement work in the National Park to tackle these type of issues.

If ever an industry was suicidal...

Later in July a spokesman for Invercauld Estate said:

> The estate became aware this morning of a press release made by the RSPB with regards to an allegation that a common gull had been caught in a trap on land at Invercauld Estate.
>
> We have spoken with the police who we understand have made enquiries and we have also undertaken our own internal investigation. We understand the police have not found evidence of illegal activity and our own enquiry has led to a similar conclusion.
>
> Nevertheless, we are extremely concerned by such an allegation and condemn outright any unlawful activity on Estate property. Our staff have been well trained in the law relating to moorland management and remain vigilant to any illegal activity whether this is intended to discredit the grouse industry or for other reasons.

What an incredible statement! There is no way the police could have said that there was no evidence of illegal activity: there was the evidence of the people who found the gull in the trap, the evidence of the SSPCA who attended to the injured bird plus the evidence of the police, SSPCA and RSPB during the search, all of whom would be able to say that there was evidence that other illegal traps had been set, albeit they had been removed. Not only has the estate denied this clear evidence but they have inferred that someone else had set the trap or traps to discredit the grouse industry.

This makes it all the more remarkable that the estate gamekeepers managed to find all the traps that 'had been set by others'. They had also removed them rather than locate them and preserve the scene until the police arrived, giving them a chance to identify which scoundrel had been trying to cause trouble for the estate.

It is little wonder that the excuses given by game management for criminal activity should be taken with a pinch of salt. When the Hell are they going to start to put their hands up when they are caught out and try to root out the criminals in their midst?

Roseanna Cunningham obviously identifies evidence of a crime here and even takes it a step further, saying in a press release,

> All forms of wildlife crime are unacceptable and I condemn the illegal use of spring traps wherever it takes place. In Deeside, the use of them has resulted in tremendous suffering for a gull which had to be euthanised. It is difficult to see their use as anything other than a blatant and criminal attempt to target protected birds of prey. The Scottish Government takes this issue extremely seriously and I urge anyone with any information about criminal activity intending to harm our wildlife to contact Police Scotland.

In the weeks following the trapping incident there were persistent rumours that a gamekeeper had been sacked from the estate. There has been no further public update from the estate by way of apology for either the actions of any of their staff or their almost unbelievable statement. Will a case have been submitted by the police to the procurator fiscal?

My Evidence to the Westminster Enquiry on Driven Grouse Shooting

During 2016 Mark Avery launched a petition to ban driven grouse shooting. Written evidence was submitted to the Petitions Committee of the Westminster Government by a range of organisations and individuals, both for and against this proposal. The following was the author's written submission:

> My background is as a police officer in Scotland. I was involved in various aspects of policing for 50 years, dealing with poachers in my earlier years and during the last 20 years as force wildlife crime officer, initially as a serving officer and latterly in

a civilian role. For the last three years I worked as an intelligence officer with the National Wildlife Crime Unit.

As a young man I went grouse beating, helped gamekeepers and indeed shot grouse. I was a great supporter of gamekeepers until relatively recently, but the volume of wildlife crime I saw that was clearly committed in the name of game management astonished me. I tried hard to integrate keepers into the Partnership for Action against Wildlife Crime, which meant I was then shunned by some conservationists. I shrugged that off but could see from policing and NWCU intelligence that on driven grouse moors, in particular those under sporting agents, the level of wildlife crime continued and showed no signs of abating.

The crimes I encountered or dealt with ranged from the killing by various means of golden eagles, white-tailed eagles, peregrines, red kites, goshawks, buzzards, ravens, badgers and otters to the illegal shooting of deer to reduce the tick burden on grouse. On one driven grouse moor all the deer were shot at night in a spotlight and the carcasses left on the hill. On another driven grouse moor the native trees beside hill burns were cut down to prevent the roosting or nesting of any birds that might predate grouse. Intelligence consistently showed that the worst areas were east and south-west Scotland and the north of England, *all areas of driven grouse moors*. Considering I was once part of the 'shooting scene' and used to shoot game this has completely sickened me.

The regular discoveries of poisonous baits or their victims present a real risk of serious injury or even death to anyone encountering and touching them. Most are found on driven grouse moors and sooner or later will lead to a fatality. In Scotland in the last five years at least eight satellite-tagged golden eagles have 'gone missing' in areas of grouse moors. This, together with a considerable number of hen harriers that have also 'gone missing' in grouse moor areas in Scotland and the north of England, strongly indicates there is no let-up in criminality.

The Scottish Parliament has made great strides forward in improving wildlife law. Examples are vicarious liability, adding the term 'reckless' as an option to 'intentional' for most wildlife crimes, upgrading snaring legislation and extending time bars for court proceeding to three years from the date of the crime. Nevertheless, despite these welcome changes, it remains almost impossible to gain a conviction for wildlife crimes committed on the vast expanse of grouse moors with multiple gamekeepers. Many landowners, sporting agents and gamekeepers on driven grouse moors are well aware of this and completely ignore the law, with the situation being considerably worse in England since the Conservative Westminster Parliament is very strongly influenced by MPs heavily involved in game shooting.

The grouse shooting lobby may try to argue that if grouse shooting is banned then many people would be out of work and the local economy would suffer. This need not be the case. There is a variety of uses for moorland, including re-wilding, that will be far better explained by others than I could ever attempt. The grouse shooting lobby try to argue that running a moor for driven grouse shooting is better for the wading birds that (should) nest there. Some driven grouse moors I have been on are almost barren of wildlife apart from red grouse, and certainly very few – if any – raptors. Many of these moors are in national parks where visitors expect to see an even bigger variety of wildlife than elsewhere. The current publicity created by wildlife crime together with a limited range of species of interest must negatively affect visitors' impression of national parks and will adversely affect local economy. Wildlife tourism could potentially bring in much more to local economies than ever grouse shooting did.

Genuine hard-working hill farmers are well deserving of CAP payments – maybe even increased CAP payments. I have been privy to the vast sums of money given to some grouse moor owners as CAP payments. Many are already millionaires and are being given money – my money as a tax payer – to run a few sheep which are there primarily to mop up ticks that might otherwise find their way on to grouse. I object as strongly to this as I do to some of these estates running rings around the law. Whether they like it or not we live in the 21ˢᵗ century, not the 19ᵗʰ century and the killing of protected species is reprehensible and does the reputation of the UK incredible harm. The Westminster Government has been virtually aiding and abetting wildlife criminals for years and it is time they realised the sway of public opinion against driven grouse shooting, the direct cause of so much wildlife crime. Warnings and compromise have been tried many times and failed.

I never thought I would ever say this, but it is time to completely ban driven grouse shooting.

Evidence to Westminster and Scottish Parliament on Driven Grouse Shooting

OCTOBER 2016 – The responses to Mark Avery's proposed ban on driven grouse shooting –which gained an incredible 123,077 signatures – and the proposal by Logan Steele on behalf of Scottish Raptor Study Groups (SRSG) to licence game shooting were published. Many of the responses in favour of either of these proposals are compelling, and there was no convincing counter-argument that Mark or SRSG are on the wrong track.

The most knowledgeable and convincing argument to ban driven grouse shooting came from Guy Shorrock, senior investigations officer with RSPB. His evidence is based on many years of experience in the field. Guy writes:

The National Crime Agency (NCA) define organised crime as 'serious crime planned, coordinated and conducted by people working together on a continuing basis. Their motivation is often, but not always, financial gain. Organised criminals working together for a particular criminal activity or activities are called an organised crime group'. The current levels of raptor persecution on driven grouse moor estates should be classed as organised crime.

Logan Steele, the spokesperson for SRSG said to the Scottish committee when giving his evidence that driven grouse shooting is a *business underpinned by criminality*.

Both are absolutely correct. The killing, not just of birds of prey but of protected mammals such as badgers and otters, is most certainly in many cases organised crime. This criminality increases the profits of the estates through the elimination of factors that would have a negative impact on grouse. The extent is difficult to prove but if anyone involved in the management of a driven grouse moor is eventually charged the police would also be considering an investigation using proceeds of crime legislation. Guy also says:

> I am aware of one individual who has been involved in grouse moor management for many years. Based on a huge amount of information, I believe this individual is one of the very top wildlife criminals in the UK, and managing gamekeepers who are responsible for the death of literally thousands of raptors and other protected wildlife during the last two decades or more. However, the reality is that this individual has never even been in a police station for an interview let alone anywhere near a court. It seems this individual, and much of the industry they are part of, consider, and with good reason, that they are pretty much untouchable.

Sporting Agents

There are several sporting agents employed by landowners to bring uplands where driven grouse shooting used to take place back to their former 'glory'. At least two such individuals are notorious, no doubt one being the same person to whom Guy Shorrock alludes. Over many years one has been described by several people as the top wildlife criminal in the UK. In their operations in Scotland and the north of England their methods, both immoral and illegal, have been the principal factor in causing these two petitions to appear before the Westminster and the Scottish parliaments. Their methods of bringing on huge grouse stocks have been praised by many landowners, gamekeepers and shooting organisations for the past decade, but at the same time several landowners and former gamekeepers have related the full and disgusting story, chapter and verse.

Apart from one gamekeeper, they were too frightened to stand up in court and be counted. The one lengthy, horrifying and convincing statement noted and signed could therefore not be corroborated. More recently the tide has started to turn as the negative publicity of the criminality and the public anger were recognised by the more reasonable and sensible folks involved in the game shooting industry.

Had more intelligence been passed to the police that would have been a good start. Had evidence been given by the older gamekeepers who were ousted to be replaced by young compliant keepers that would have been a great step towards a court case. Had much more support been given to the gamekeepers who had been (or were being) encouraged or directed to carry out criminal acts, they could have provided evidence (as opposed to intelligence) in the form of witness statements or the recovery of illegal items and a case could most certainly have been submitted for prosecution. This could have been achievable by the concerted action of the various shooting and land-owning organisations that have pretty much buried their collective heads in the sand for years, with no public acknowledgement and only half-hearted condemnation of what is taking place. The extent of the criminality, if proved, could have culminated in a considerable jail sentence.

Even in 2017, using the common law charge of conspiracy (which is not time-limited as are statutory offences), it is still not too late for this to happen.

The Oral Evidence

18 OCTOBER 2016 – Evidence for the on-line petition to ban driven grouse shooting initiated by Dr Mark Avery was heard by the Petitions Committee of the Westminster Parliament. Oral evidence for the petition was given by Mark Avery and Jeff Knott, head of nature policy at RSPB. Evidence against the petition was given by Amanda Anderson, director of the Moorland Association, and Liam Stokes, head of shooting, The Countryside Alliance.

Mark opened with a very clear and eloquent statement:

> Driven grouse shooting has five main problems with it. It has animal welfare problems, nature conservation problems, wider environmental problems, wildlife crime problems and problems of social inequity. That is a unique combination of problems. They do not apply to other aspects of shooting. I feel, and clearly 123,000 other people feel, that something has to change. The driven grouse shooting industry has shown no sign of wanting to reform. It is up to Parliament to create that change. Perhaps slightly naïvely, I believe in parliamentary democracy. I believe that, if the people bring a strong enough case to Parliament, then Parliament should act. That is why I am here.

He elaborated in respect of driven grouse shooting as distinct from any other form of grouse shooting:

> This is a very specific hobby. That is all that driven grouse shooting is: shooting birds for fun, which I believe has benefits for a few but disbenefits for the wider public and for the environment. I do not see any way of tinkering with it, so that is why I would like to see it banned.

From the reading of the questions in the transcript Mark Avery and Jeff Knott were examined most intensely, while Amanda

Anderson and Liam Stokes had a somewhat easy ride.

The debate took place in the Westminster Hall on 31 October. Most of the participating MPs were Conservative and a number of them were closely linked with shooting. They were rude, dismissive and appeared completely contemptuous of the fact that more than 123,000 people had concerns serious enough to enable this debate to take place. The chair, who should have been unbiased, was extremely disrespectful and visibly of a view that the debate was a complete waste of time.

It was never considered for a minute that a Conservative government would – or ever will – ban driven grouse shooting. For anyone having read the written evidence or listened to the oral evidence the duty of the MPs was at least to take account of public concern. They could have acquiesced (even reluctantly) that there is indeed something far wrong on driven grouse moors, and agreed that wildlife legislation in England and Wales is woefully inadequate compared to that of Scotland and urgently in need of change to attempt to curb the type of criminality set out before them. The whole debate, which was meant to exemplify democracy at its best, was a disgraceful sham.

The MPs in the Westminster debate were in complete contrast to the Public Petitions Committee of the Scottish Parliament which took the oral evidence on 27 October 2016 in relation to the petition by Logan Steele of Scottish Raptor Study Groups to licence all game bird shooting in Scotland. Logan, along with the other witnesses, Andrea Hudspeth (Tayside Raptor Study Group) and Duncan Orr-Ewing (Head of Species & Land Management, RSPB Scotland), were treated fairly and respectfully by all members of the committee. On 8 December Dr Colin Shedden, director in Scotland of BASC, and Tim Baynes, director of the Scottish Moorland Group gave evidence against licensing to the committee. Both were treated with equal courtesy.

Returning to the Westminster debate, it was obvious that the Parliamentary Under-Secretary of State for Environment,

Food and Rural Affairs, Dr Therese Coffey, had her conclusion written days in advance. Like the remainder of the Conservative MPs present, (three of whom had knighthoods, though manners certainly never came into any of the reasons for bestowing this honour upon them), Dr Coffey showed absolutely no interest in trying to address criminality on driven grouse moors. She was steadfastly of the view that the continuation of grouse shooting is best for everyone, though anyone with any gumption sees that the only gain is to a handful of people, part of which is made up of the conservative group participating in the debate. She also appeared to speak for every MP present at the debate, despite some with completely opposing views. She concluded the debate by the following disgraceful statement:

> I will finish by stating that the Government have no intention of banning driven grouse shooting, but we have every intention of bringing to justice those who break the law. We all agree that conserving the upland moorlands is in everyone's best interests. We will help to ensure that a constructive dialogue continues so that grouse shooting is protected and these valuable moorlands thrive.

This statement illustrates that we'll wait long enough for the law in England and Wales to be made sufficiently robust to convict those who kill raptors on driven grouse moors, those servant gamekeepers who act for their criminal masters. Killing by proxy.

An Interesting Week in the Fight Against Wildlife Crime

4 MARCH 2017 – It was an interesting week in the fight against wildlife crime. What the Scottish Government makes of the review on game bird hunting regulations in other European countries and on satellite-tagged raptors, a review sparked by the disappearance of so many satellite-tagged golden eagles and hen harriers, is eagerly awaited.

To her credit, the Cabinet Secretary for the Environment had been doing the rounds, speaking at the Scottish Raptor Study Groups' Annual Conference in Perth on 25 February and, at the opposite end of the wildlife crime debate, to the annual conference of the Scottish Gamekeepers' Association on 3 March, again in Perth.

This was Ms Cunningham's message on raptor persecution to the gamekeepers, as reported in *The Courier*:

> I have no patience at all with old fashioned attitudes towards these birds that linger on in this day and age. We all have to abide by the law, and must do so every day.

> I have no truck with any excuse that raptors damage driven grouse shooting interests – such damage is a business risk that grouse moor owners have to live with, and manage for – and this has to be done within the law.

So, meaningful wording and, at last, a real message that the Scottish Government considers any threats to grouse from raptors no more than a business risk they have to accept. Will this message be taken on board if new applications are made to SNH for licences to control/cull/shoot (kill by any other name) buzzards?

The Cabinet Secretary's warning to the gamekeepers gives some hope that when all the evidence has been assimilated and assessed by the Scottish Government something significant might transpire to eliminate – or at least seriously reduce – raptor persecution.

Tethered Eagle Owl 'Lure' on Lammermuirs

APRIL 2017 – An intriguing story on the blog *Raptor Persecution UK*. It appears that a man with a quad bike and a shotgun was seen at the edge of a shelter belt on the Lammermuirs. Tethered on a post within shotgun range of the shelter belt was an eagle owl. The man made off with the eagle owl when he saw he was being filmed.

There was much discussion on the blog as to whether or not a crime had been committed.

Over at least the last ten years quite a number of grouse moor keepers are keeping eagle owls. They're committing no offence in doing so but a suspicious mind suggests they are for use in luring in birds that the keepers want to shoot.

The law (Wildlife and Countryside Act 1981 as amended) in this respect states:

5.–(1) Subject to the provisions of this Part, if any person –

(d) uses as a decoy, for the purpose of killing or taking any wild bird, any sound recording or *any live bird or other animal whatever which is tethered*, or which is secured by means of braces or other similar appliances, or which is blind, maimed or injured;

(f) knowingly causes or permits to be done an act which is mentioned in the foregoing provisions of this subsection and which is not lawful under subsection (5),

he shall be guilty of an offence.

The man was almost certainly intent on decoying birds to shoot. The species of bird intended to be shot is not relevant, it is the tethering of the eagle owl for this purpose that constitutes the crime. However, without any other evidence of shots being heard, empty cartridges on the ground or dead or injured birds it's unlikely a prosecutor would proceed with a case.

Having said that, if we look at the elements of circumstantial evidence the case is not too far short:

- Motive: Get rid of 'problem' birds from the moor
- Ability: Presumably the man has permission to shoot (he certainly will if he is the keeper), he has a shotgun and

(presumably) ammunition
- Guilty Intention: This element is unknown
- Identification: Unknown, but may be determined by police investigation
- Conduct after the Crime: Gathered owl and sped off when he was aware he was being filmed
- Opportunity: Unknown until after any interview. If the man is identified this element is complete (as opposed to him having been on holiday, having a broken leg or some other reason he could not have been at the scene)
- Preparation: Eagle owl tethered to post, plus shotgun and transport

Unfortunately, in the absence of other crucial evidence showing intent it's unlikely that the eagle owl could be considered a 'decoy'; it was simply an eagle owl tethered to a post, the use of which is unable to be confirmed.

There is also Section 18 of the Act, which states:

(1)   Any person who attempts to commit an offence under the foregoing provisions of this Part shall be guilty of an offence and shall be punishable in like manner as for the said offence.

(2)   Any person who for the purposes of committing an offence under the foregoing provisions of this Part, has in his possession anything capable of being used for committing the offence shall be guilty of an offence and shall be punishable in like manner as for the said offence.

He has not yet 'attempted' to commit an offence. Since there is no direct evidence of what the man intended to do with the owl, the gun and the cartridges (even though everyone knows) this also falls short of the evidence required for section 18(2). Critics should always be mindful, even if the man was subsequently identified by the police, that evidence to convict must be 'beyond reasonable doubt'. The action taken should have been:

- Report the incident to the police *at the time*. Regrettably there has been so much misinformation on social media about the police not being interested or being corrupt that some people are likely to have been put off reporting suspicious wildlife incidents to the police. These views do not help to solve wildlife crime and most certainly work to the criminals' advantage.
- The police could have investigated the allegation and traced and interviewed the suspect. He would be unlikely to make any admission but still worth a try. Whether a positive or negative outcome an intelligence entry could then be submitted.

One comment on the blog advocates reporting to the police *after* releasing details on social media; another suggests reporting first to RSPB, then to SSPCA then to the police. Thankfully the blog editors make the point very clearly that crimes should not be put into the public domain before the police are informed. Why does one sometimes get the impression that some who claim to be conservationists seem more pleased to criticise and even thwart the police rather than see a wildlife criminal caught and convicted?

As a priority we now need to get rid of this nonsense that the police are not interested in solving wildlife crime and encourage witnesses to phone the police right away. This could be addressed by an innovative campaign by the police. Phoning non-government agencies first delays the investigation, sometimes fatally. By all means phone, for instance RSPB, after phoning the police but do not put the details into the public domain until the police have had time to carry out an investigation.

As it turned out the police had been contacted, investigated the incident and spoke to the suspect. There was insufficient evidence to submit a report to the procurator fiscal.

The Blog Raptor Persecution UK

When this blog began as Raptor Persecution Scotland around 2010 it appeared, at least to the author and other wildlife crime officers, to be very critical and negative about police efforts to deal with raptor persecution. This was particularly disheartening to those who were putting in a huge amount of effort to try not only to obtain convictions but working in parallel to educate and raise awareness in relation to all types of wildlife crime.

The police view of the blog was not helped by some who commented on the items published. Some had no idea whatsoever of what powers the police had and the limits placed on searches of land, buildings or suspects. Some the criticism of the police was certainly justified but it just seemed to be the theme through many of the incidents reported. Other comments accused the police, prosecutors and courts of corruption. At one point the author was so sick and tired of the persistent negative comments that he commented himself that the blog would be better named Police Persecution Scotland.

There was certainly great value in that the blog was bringing crime related to game management into the public domain in a way that no other media or conservation body was managing to achieve. This was even more apparent, and important, when the blog changed focus to cover UK-wide raptor persecution. The purpose of this book runs along the same lines.

In more recent times the blogger has moderated considerably (or have the police improved; I'm not sure which). Credit is more regularly given for some of the investigations carried out and there is a better understanding of the difficulties in trying to police what takes place in countless acres of what remains for the purposes of surveillance as 'private' land. Reciprocal credit must go to the blog for the effort taken to dig deep into some of the issues and to report accurately. The comments remain a mixed bag of experience, common sense, bias and nonsense but that goes with the territory of allowing or encouraging comments within media of all types.

Despite still not agreeing with everything written on the blog, it has been a great help to the author – as have some other blogs, websites and media – in more easily identifying raptor and other wildlife-related crimes and incidents on which to comment and expand.

Blame the Anti-Grouse Shooting Activists (or are They Extremists?)

JUNE 2016 – In the summer edition of *The Scottish Sporting Gazette* an article was published that had been written by Tim Baynes, director of Scottish Land and Estates' Moorland Forum. The article had been discussed on the *Raptor Persecution UK* blog in June 2017. Its content, in summary, was a claim that crime against birds of prey and linked to shooting estates is 'hugely improved' and that 'the police believe that wildlife crime generally is now under control'.

There are many arguments that would counter these two statements, even more so now that the Environment Secretary is seriously considering further action against shooting estates. What was really offensive in the article was Tim's claim that:

> the problem now is that all the positive work by land managers risks being derailed by a small number of committed activists, particularly those who are anti-grouse shooting.

I read the *Raptor Persecution UK blog* subscribers' comments on the article and was surprised that no one picked up on this preposterous statement. There are most certainly activists, rightly so, trying to draw the attention of the Scottish Government and the public to wildlife crime, especially that committed on grouse moors. They are most certainly committed but it's questionable that we are talking about a small number; in fact a significant proportion of the population are disgusted at the continuing arrogance of some estates. Think of the 123,000 plus who signed Mark Avery's petition. Think also of all the negative publicity about the use of gas guns on grouse moors where raptors, particularly hen harriers, could be nesting and most recently the gas gun that was reported as operating on Glenogil Estate in Angus. This *may* not be illegal but anyone with an interest in the countryside knows its purpose. A beleaguered industry should try to comply with public opinion rather than put two fingers up. They should be trying to make friends rather than enemies.

There is indeed positive work being carried out by some land managers. If this is being derailed surely the blame lies at the door of the estate owners, sporting agents and gamekeepers who continue to kill (or are complicit in the killing of) protected species. In Scotland there are several people in some of these positions whose greed at producing the biggest possible number of grouse for driven shooting includes wiping out as many species as possible that would adversely affect grouse. Their identities are well known, and their illegal methods have featured in discussions with many land managers over the past decade. They are still operating and in fact are revered by some in the grouse industry rather than being reported to the police. Tim knows of them, yet for any alleged derailing of positive work he blames law-abiding people (that he later in his article refers to as 'extremists') who simply want the law upheld.

Coming out with transparent twaddle like this is not helpful. Admittedly the article is nearly a year old but there has been little or nothing in print from the game management industry since then that puts the blame for raptor persecution exactly where it should be focused.

Short-Eared Owl Shot at Leadhills

MAY 2017 – So another bird of prey has been shot on Leadhills Estate, Biggar. This time it was a short-eared owl, shot in broad daylight at 11.45 on 31 May by a man whose description was given by a witness and who was driving a black 4×4 with a dark canopy. In the same month a hen harrier was also shot at Leadhills in broad daylight, this time at 17.15 on 4 May. The criminal on this occasion was believed to be a man on a quad bike with his face covered. Has there been a decision to resurrect Leadhills as a driven grouse moor?

The police have appealed for information in relation to both incidents. There was a three-week delay in the publication of the most recent incident but this is understandable. When a crime is witnessed – an unusual bonus in the case of wildlife crime on grouse moors – there is a higher than normal chance of obtaining evidence against the criminal, and the police would want to carry out certain investigations before putting the crime into the public domain. They appear still to be short of the evidence they require and their appeal through the media gives a further (slight) chance of gaining more evidence. Crucially it also lets the public know what is still going on in relation to some driven grouse moors.

It is not only Leadhills that is currently the centre of police attention for wildlife crime; an investigation is also underway on Raeshaw Estate, a driven grouse moor in the Borders and, as already stated, a gas gun was photographed in use on a third driven grouse moor: Glenogil.

It is almost beyond belief that these incidents are still taking place in an industry teetering on the edge of being licensed. This disgraceful conduct affects the reputation of the decent, hard-working and law-abiding gamekeepers and landowners who will be dragged under by their criminal colleagues. The common factors with all three estates mentioned, plus several more, is that they have been hotbeds of wildlife crime for many years with a disgraceful catalogue of incidents logged against them. Coincidentally they all are or have been in the recent past managed by sporting agent Mark Osborne.

Could it be too much to hope for that, at last, shooting and landowning organisations will collectively make an approach to the landowners, sporting agents, shooting tenants or gamekeepers who are still determined to bring about the demise of driven grouse shooting. Will they also deign to pass on intelligence to Police Scotland that might allow them to put the criminals responsible before a court?

Looking ahead to licensing, it stands to reason that the strategy of a 'successful' sporting agent on one estate will be replicated on the other estates for which he has charge. Scottish Government should consider whether if a licence to manage land for game shooting is removed from one of these estates for wildlife crime can it be removed from the others. The same principle could be applied by SNH in relation to revocation of the right to use a general licence. Make them sit up and take notice.

Another Raptor Trapping Incident Confirms the Change from Poisoning

JULY 2017 – Police Scotland launched an appeal for information after the trapping of a buzzard on the south slopes of Beinn Bhreac, which is in the Monadhliaths in Inverness-shire. The RSPB report stated this is a grouse moor, which comes as no surprise, though the estate is not named.

The bird had been caught on 3 or 4 June and the trap used appeared to be baited with a dead woodpigeon. Being set amongst moss it would be easy to conceal. Before it caught the buzzard it would be completely invisible and would only be found if someone inspected the dead pigeon. The trap appeared to be a Fenn trap, though it is difficult to confirm this in the photo used by the media. It would be ingenuous to think that the trap was set by someone other than an estate employee. Since there are few predators away out on a grouse moor that cause problems for sheep farming it is reasonable to assume the person most likely to have set the trap would be a gamekeeper. Most farmers have little use for traps in any case.

That the trap was set at all beggars belief and yet again confirms the egotism of the criminal involved that (1) no one would find the trap and (2) if they did, the police would not manage to obtain evidence to link it back to him.

There were minimum responses from gamekeeping and landowning organisations apart from the usual feeble couple of lines from The Scottish Gamekeepers' Association.

These organisations know at least as well as the police who the rogues are. They must also see this as yet more evidence to convince the Scottish Government to licence shooting. So why are gamekeeping and landowning organisations doing bugger all to deter or get rid of these folks?

In the Summer 2017 edition of *Scottish Gamekeeper*, the magazine of the Scottish Gamekeepers' Association, the chairman, Alex Hogg, wrote an article in which he accepted that some gamekeepers *'have tarnished themselves and the profession.'* He rightly claims that this should not discredit all gamekeepers and that, with the threat of licensing of shooting looming *'enough is enough'.*

The exclamation *'enough is enough'* didn't seem to be directed at the killing of protected wildlife by gamekeepers: it was directed at perceived threats *against* gamekeepers.

Hogg claims that *'law abiding people will be at the mercy of the extreme fringe that want nothing other than grouse shooting stopped. For them, the removal of a few licences (and a few gamekeepers and their families) is a means to an end; a stepping-stone'.*

He questioned, with remarkable naivety, *'I wonder how we have got to this'.*

It is abundantly clear how this position has been reached.

What is also abundantly clear is that at the same rate as the poisoning of raptors is reducing, the use of Fenn traps set with baits is increasing. This is obviously the replacement method of controlling raptors.

A comment on the *Raptor Persecution UK* blog report on the trapping of this buzzard revealed that police powers in relation to searches of 'private' land may not be widely known. The person commenting wrote:

> Are the police doing random checks to ensure compliance? I'd love to see the stats on that? The number of registered trap users who have been inspected? Sadly...probably not available because it's probably not being done. So really they are not doing anything other than responding to complaints when the public report these very hard to detect crimes.

Firstly, Fenn traps do not need to be registered with the police; registration is limited to corvid cage traps and snares. Neither can the police do random checks to ensure compliance with any type of 'pest' control. A police officer can only justify entering land to inspect any of these traps when there is reasonable suspicion that they are being used illegally.

When Scottish Government get around to licensing, which now seems inevitable, it would be prudent to factor in a power to allow the police to inspect pest control methods as a condition of the licence.

SNH Events – A Walk on a Sporting Estate in Glenisla

JULY 2017 – The following event was advertised in the latest edition of *Scottish Wildlife Trust Events and Activities July – November 2017*:

> Sun 30 July, 2.00–4.00pm Glen Isla Sporting Estate Visit
>
> A guided visit to a sporting estate in Glen Isla with the gamekeeper. Meet at Fergus (NO193682). Turn right off the B951 past Forter Castle.

The estate is not named on the SWT booklet but several comments appeared on social media criticising Scottish Wildlife Trust for organising such a visit.

While the author regularly knocks several sporting estates, especially grouse moors, and supports the need to licence grouse moors (or indeed ban driven grouse shooting altogether) game shooting is currently legal and it is neither correct nor fair to dismiss a guided tour of an estate out of hand without knowing if any criminal activity has taken place there. There are many grouse moors that should be afforded no credibility whatsoever but on the other hand there have been guided tours by responsible gamekeepers in the past where those taking part have been seriously impressed with what has been seen and by the knowledge of the gamekeeper.

From the author's examples on one grouse moor in Angus he was shown nesting barn owls and nesting kestrels. He also saw many buzzards flying around plus a rare bird on many estates: a goshawk. On a Perthshire grouse moor that was also rearing grey partridges he saw an even wider variety of raptors that included hen harrier, golden eagle and red kite, and was also amazed at the knowledge the keeper had of tree species and wild plants. On a low-ground Perthshire shoot he is aware of several pairs of nesting buzzards, at least two pairs of nesting ospreys and at least one pair of nesting red kites. Lastly, on the Highland Perthshire estate on which he did a year-long survey and on which his book *A Wealth of Wildlife* is based, he identified 90 species of birds including hen harrier, white-tailed eagle, tawny owl, nesting red kites and many nesting buzzards. Golden eagle, peregrine and merlin were also regular visitors that had been seen both before and after the year's study but their visits unfortunately never coincided with the days of the survey.

To dismiss all shooting estates and gamekeepers out of hand is wrong. There are some that, because of the owner, the sporting agent or the gamekeepers, don't warrant the time of day. Conversely there are some where, even though the habitat is managed for grouse and could be altered to be of more value to other species, a walk with the gamekeeper can be incredibly enlightening.

Until the identity of the estate is known it is unfair to be judgemental.

The SWT person leading the estate visit commented afterwards:

> Thank you, Alan for your support. The members of the local SWT group had a great day on the hill at Fergus. The head keeper was a mine of information on the local wildlife. Careful management of the heather has resulted in a rich diverse turf that supports lower numbers of deer but in much better condition, twin fawns are common, lots of blue hares, breeding golden plovers and many other species. What is so important is maintaining the balance of nature and a well-managed estate can be so much more diverse than when overgrazed by sheep. We are well aware that some neighbouring estates are not managed so well. Enlightened land usage benefits us all.

'Pest Control' Practices Filmed in the Peak District National Park

JULY 2017 – *The Mirror* newspaper and other sources alerted readers to a short film put together by a group known as the Hunt Investigation Team (HIT). This team had been filming covertly on Moscar Estate, a grouse moor in the Peak District National Park owned by the Duke of Rutland, and had put together film of a series of activities by men they described as the estate gamekeepers.

The team claimed that there are around 400 snares, presumably set for foxes rather than rabbits or hares, on the estate. This is a huge number of snares to check daily but experience shows that many of these driven grouse moors employ seven or eight gamekeepers, often under the control of a sporting agent rather than the estate owner. Nevertheless it is hard to believe that every snare is checked within the legal time frame.

The film shows many traps, snares and incidents that most folks would think are illegal, but in fact are legal if used or carried out with the permission of the landowner or agent. Some, though, may well be illegal and the police officers carrying out the investigation will have a much better idea after speaking to the witnesses and viewing the full range of film and photos. At first glance the Hunt Investigation Team (HIT) may have filmed or photographed the following offences.

A photograph of a snare set on a track looks suspiciously like an illegal locking snare. It is an old-style snare of the type with an option of two holes to complete the loop. If the wire is passed through one hole it runs freely, but if it is passed through the alternative hole, the snare locks when tightened. With any luck the police will have been made aware and recovered the snares before details went public and the evidence disappeared. If the footage was released in advance of notification to the police, the Hunt Investigation Team will probably have wasted their surveillance effort.

There is a shocking sequence of a badger in a snare being released by a man with a semi-automatic shotgun. He fires two shots right beside the badger's head to cut the snare. The badger runs off along a path and immediately runs into another snare. This time there are five or six shots from the shotgun in a botched attempt to free it, but the snare has eventually to be sliced with a spade.

While badgers will not be the easiest animals to free from a snare, breaking the snare by shooting it is wild west stuff and certainly not the way to do it. It almost certainly needs two people, one to secure the badger, probably with a forked stick, and the other to cut through the part of the snare that is round the badger's neck, or slacken the snare and remove it completely.

Obtaining proof that the badger in the film eventually ran off with two snares round its neck that are extremely unlikely to ever come off and would ultimately kill the badger would be hard to obtain but this would be the most likely outcome. This may not be unusual; a senior member of the Scottish Gamekeepers' Association once commented at a meeting that if he caught a badger he would simply cut the snare and allow the badger to run off and take its chance. A non-target animal being caught in a snare is not a nuisance, it is an unfortunate victim that, provided it is not severely injured because of its capture, deserves to be released in the best possible condition to survive.

Easier to prove is that the badger is subjected to acute stress by these shots being set off right beside its head. They would be absolutely deafening and, since the badger is captive and temporarily under the control of man and being subjected to unnecessary suffering, this is likely to be a contravention of Section 4 of the Animal Welfare Act 2006. The shots may also have damaged the badger's hearing irreparably. If the snares used were indeed locking snares it is almost certain that, being left on the badger's neck, they would kill it within a relatively short time. It would have great difficulty breathing and would be unlikely to be able to swallow.

The HIT team further claim that a badger was shot and buried in a wood. If that is the case it should be recoverable by the police provided they were informed before the story was made public. A post mortem examination should confirm the cause of death.

Another part of the film shows a jay in a Fenn trap. It seems that the jay is the decoy bird rather than a bird that had been caught in the trap. It is completely illegal to use a jay as a decoy bird in Scotland. In the equivalent general licence that applies to England the jay is not included as a decoy species, however another current government document *does* include a jay as a decoy species. This type of discrepancy cropped up in Scotland years ago in relation to multi-catch corvid cage traps. General licences were issued at that time by two different departments and the content was different. The prosecutor, rightly, did not proceed with the case as it was obvious the accused would claim he was using the document that suited him. The same will be the case with jays in traps in England.

The gamekeepers in the film were wearing masks, plus one was wearing nitrile gloves. They were reminiscent of criminals about to carry out an armed robbery. It is also extremely worrying that we have masked men carrying shotguns around in the countryside. What must decent gamekeepers and their representative organisations think of this film? They must be totally disgusted. Hopefully the estate will get a visit in due course from one of the organisations and if the duke is anywhere near worthy of the title he'll get rid of the whole bunch who have brought almost unprecedented disgrace to gamekeeping.

The Hunt Investigation Team are of the view that foxes are a minority percentage of the captures. They accept that foxes are a legal target but claim that snares are routinely set in active badger territory.

They claim that snares are being used to target mountain hares in the Peak District, and often set in the most active hare territory. This is ostensibly to control the risk of louping ill infection, but allege that the local incidence of this is virtually zero, with a hare in a snare and filmed by them being perfectly healthy. The team's perceived logic is that hares attract foxes and foxes compromise grouse.

It transpires that in early September 2017 the police did manage to prepare a case and send it to the Crown Prosecution Service. The charges are not known though it is highly likely that one of the main charges would be a cruelty charge under the Animal Welfare Act 2006 for discharging a shotgun numerous times right beside the terrified badger's ear then allowing it to run off with two snares round its neck.

On 1 October 2017 a BBC news report stated that the Crown Prosecution Service decided no charges would be brought. Before looking at possible reasons why, it is worth contemplating the view of the owners of Moscar Estate, the Duke and Duchess of Rutland. The BBC news item reported that they were 'horrified by the allegations'. Does that mean they were horrified by what was filmed happening to the badger? I bet it doesn't; the wording used indicates they were horrified that there was an allegation that one of their staff could be suspected of breaking the law.

It is also worth contemplating the quote from a spokesman for the estate: 'Endangered birds like curlew and lapwing are flourishing in grouse moors because gamekeepers do such a good job at protecting them from foxes.' Maybe so, but for balance he omitted to say that endangered hen harriers were virtually non-existent on grouse moors because gamekeepers do such a good job of killing them.

Returning to CPS dropping the case, why would this be?

Was it not in the public interest? Surely the answer to that is that it is very much in the public interest. Deliberate cruelty to a trapped animal plus a man wearing a mask and with a shotgun.

Was there insufficient evidence? This is hard to say without knowing all the facts. The incidents were filmed, the film should have been submitted to the police without breaks or cutting, and showing a time and date. It is also unlikely that there was only one observer, since it would be risky for the Hunt Investigation Team only to field one person for a job in the middle of moorland and where firearms may be a factor. There may well therefore have been corroboration.

Was the person with the mask and shotgun not identified? It is likely that he was, and that he was interviewed by the police. Positive identification for court purposes might depend on whether the police managed to get round the fact that the man was masked, especially if he made 'No comment' responses to questioning, as most gamekeepers are advised to do. The decision on whether there is sufficient evidence of identification to take a case to court is ultimately that of the prosecutor.

Did the CPS decline to use film or the evidence that was obtained covertly? There have been precedents where covert surveillance taken by NGOs has been accepted, especially in England. However there is a real mixed message with covert filming since, if this was the reason the case was not proceeded with, it is at least the second case this year in England plus a further two in Scotland.

The Fate of Nesting Marsh Harriers on Our Uplands

MAY 2017 – RSPB staff, acting under a licence, found a marsh harrier nest on Denton Moor, which is near Ilkley, in Wharfedale, North Yorkshire. Marsh harriers normally nest in reed beds and it is unusual to find one nesting on heather moorland. The nest had five eggs and in order to monitor the birds' nesting success RSPB investigations officers placed a hidden camera with a view of the nest. On 19 May the eggs had disappeared from the nest, though there was still a pair of marsh harriers in the general area.

The film footage showed the following:

- 1240 on 17 May a bang was heard and a few seconds later the female marsh harrier came off the nest. There was a further bang, some shouting and the noise of the revving of a vehicle
- 1242 a man with a shotgun approaches the nest then walks back in the opposite direction
- Surprisingly after this disturbance the female harrier returned to the nest
- 13.56 the female flies up off the nest again, almost immediately followed by four shots, Seconds later two men with their faces covered and carrying shotguns walk to the nest then continue on out of view towards where the bird had flown, then returned to the nest. One of the men bends down and may have removed one of the eggs. They are heard commenting on how much down there is at the nest.
- 0941 on 18 May a man returns, again with a shotgun and is believed to have removed a further egg or eggs from the nest.

On 10 August 2017 North Yorkshire Police, presumably after their initial investigations, circulate a press release regarding the incident. Simultaneously the relevant video clips are released by RSPB Investigations.

It is reasonable to infer that the two men firing off four shots was an attempt to shoot the harrier. The fact that a pair of harriers was still in the area a couple of days later tends to put some doubt on their shooting skills. They may just have wanted to prevent the birds breeding though that could have been done with equal effect by simply removing the eggs. The men had obviously seen a harrier's nest (probably that of a hen harrier) in the past, since part of their conversation in relation to the amount of down around the nest was to the effect that 'you'd think there was fucking young uns there'. This comment refers to the amount of down that builds up on the heather around a harrier nest as the fledglings moult down to grow feathers.

In the police press release the men are describe as wearing dull, brownish green coloured jackets, traditional country caps, and carrying what looked like shotguns and a brown game bag. The man who appeared on the second day was similarly dressed and carrying a green rucksack. The sound of the vehicle which had been revving is believed to have been a quad bike.

This was an excellent piece of work by RSPB Investigations. Whether or not the footage will be used in a court case or whether it would even be accepted by the Crown Prosecution Service it serves to show exactly what is happening on our uplands. How many times is a similar scene played out every year and never witnessed? Since the press release it is believed that at least one person has contacted the police and given a name for one of the men involved.

An RSPB blog on the incident reports that in North Yorkshire *during the last ten years, within five miles of the marsh harrier nesting attempt, we know of at least nine red kites which have been illegally poisoned and a further three shot*.

And the Westminster Government sit on their hands and do nothing to change legislation. On no, sorry, that's not quite true, they had hoped to repeal the hunting legislation…

Some Wise Words from Glen Tanar Estate

OCTOBER 2017 – It is heartening to finish this section on a positive note as a result of a blog entitled Managing Grouse at Glen Tanar written by Colin McClean, the estate's wildlife manager.

Glen Tanar estate is located on the eastern side of the Cairngorms National Park, within an area that includes many intensively managed grouse moors. It covers 25,000 acres and provides holiday cottages, grouse shooting, deer stalking, fishing, wildlife safaris, wildlife photography, walking and mountain biking and photography. With such a range of activities grouse shooting is much lower on the list than elsewhere, with some of their shooting carried out over pointers.

The first point of interest is that Colin's role is referred to as a wildlife manager rather than a gamekeeper. It is likely that this encompasses a far wider scope of wildlife care and habitat management than simply trying to encourage huge numbers of grouse so that hundreds can be shot at each shooting day. The role is described as 'designed to try and balance the nature conservation interests of an internationally important wildlife site with the economically important sporting interests of a traditional Highland estate'.

In a paragraph on hen harriers the estate claim to have been the only estate to have provided supplementary food for hen harriers and then successfully driven grouse in the same year. He reckoned that the supplementary feeding, at a nest of three chicks, reduced predation on grouse chicks by some 200 young grouse. While not excusing the killing of hen harriers by gamekeepers on many driven grouse moors this demonstrates why they do it. Colin rightly boasts of 'having successfully driven grouse in a year when 13 raptor species (including owls) all successfully bred and fledged young'.

The conclusion of the article is the part that is refreshing honest as a public statement from anyone involved in grouse shooting:

> Big bags are not essential and most of our guests are happy to spend a day chatting to friends in beautiful surroundings while watching the dogs tirelessly work. Perhaps only 10–20 birds will be shot.

But amidst the chat and the income, the debate surrounding grouse shooting rages on. Jobs and economy on one side, raptor persecution on the other. Political scrutiny is now intense. For me there is little political threat to grouse shooting provided the sector obeys the law of the land. There are far too many jobs involved for politicians to take action lightly. However, obeying the law is a must and this remains a challenge for some. The recent review of satellite tagging of golden eagles shows an unambiguous pattern of regular disappearances above grouse moors when they rarely disappear over anywhere else. For me it's not the RSPB or campaigners like Chris Packham or Mark Avery who threaten grouse shooting. They are just campaigning for the law to be obeyed. The threat to grouse shooting comes from those who refuse to abide by the law and continue to persecute raptors. If a ban ever does come about, then the responsibility for losing all the traditions, all the economy and all the jobs will lie entirely at their door.

The majority of Colin McLean's statements are borne out by the incidents described this book, and the only one worth challenging is the economic argument that 'there are far too many jobs involved for politicians to take action lightly'.

PART 5

The Future

A wide range of wildlife crime has been discussed in these pages: animal cruelty, crime related to shooting estates and in particular that on driven grouse moors. The treatment of crime associated with driven grouse moors is the most expansive since it is that activity that undoubtedly is responsible for the most serious of raptor-related crimes. Dialogue with organisations representing landowners and gamekeepers has been tried through regional and local PAW groups, with limited success. The answer may be licensing or it may be the ultimate solution of a complete ban on the practice of driven grouse shooting.

Examples have also been provided on how other organisations and experts can be of invaluable help in police investigations – the investigation of wildlife crime, in fact, probably utilises a wider range of expertise than almost any other type of crime investigation.

Through the training and use of specialist officers, variously referred to as wildlife crime officers, wildlife crime liaison officers or rural crime officers, often assisted or advised by the UK National Wildlife Crime Unit, the investigation of wildlife crime has improved considerably. With more specialist prosecutors, convictions are more likely. If impact statements are included as standard in police reports to the prosecutor as information for the court, penalties are likely to be more realistic. Through the work of the various working groups within the Partnership for Action against Wildlife Crime (PAW) good progress has been made with forensic work and training, less so with awareness-raising and raptor persecution. The Scottish legislation has been tightened quite considerably, though in England and Wales there seems to be a real reluctance to do so.

If prospects in England and Wales look bleak and disheartening, the future in Scotland has more promise, but government reviews and developments still await final decisions and action. So where do we go from here in dealing with wildlife crime, particularly on driven grouse moors?

England and Wales:
Improvements that Should be Considered

The Westminster Government in 2017 appear so protective of their landowning colleagues that their lack of any action to prevent or detect wildlife crime, particularly on grouse moors is nothing short of a disgrace. Even with the difficulties for the police in obtaining sufficient evidence to convict a suspect of many of the wildlife crimes the police are having to operate with legislation that is totally unsuitable for the purpose. How about the Westminster Government at last atoning and considering the following legislative amendments?

1. Wildlife and Countryside Act – Wild Birds

Under the Wildlife and Countryside Act 1981 in England and Wales Section 1(1) states:

*Subject to the provisions of this Part, if any person **intentionally***
(a) kills, injures or takes any wild bird;
(aa) takes, damages or destroys a nest of a wild bird included in Schedule ZA1 (eagles and osprey)
(b) takes, damages or destroys the nest of any wild bird while that nest is in use or being built; or
(c) takes or destroys an egg of any wild bird, he shall be guilty of an offence.

There is an easy get out of jail free card with this wording if, for example, a suspect who had shot a bird, say, a buzzard, maintains he thought it was some other bird that can legally be shot, say, a woodpigeon (this is based on an actual case in Scotland before the law was changed). It could be extremely difficult to prove beyond reasonable doubt that there was *intent* to shoot the buzzard. If he failed to identify it properly before shooting, a court may hold that it is a *reckless* act but was not intentional. A Not Guilty verdict follows.

There are countless other examples, which shows the need for the wording to be changed to *intentionally or recklessly.*

2. Wildlife and Countryside Act – Powers of Search

Police officers in England and Wales, when they deal with pesticide investigations, are still having to work under legislation that was really written to be enforced by the Pesticide Safety Directorate or Natural England under the Wildlife Incident Investigation Scheme. The relevant offences in these pieces of legislation from the 1960s govern misuse and storage, with relatively low penalties. If the pesticides most regularly abused for the poisoning of wildlife were to be incorporated into the Wildlife and Countryside Act the penalties and powers for the police would be identical to those in other sections of the Act. Investigation would be much simpler, convictions easier to obtain and penalties more appropriate to the offences.

In England and Wales powers without warrant under Section 19 of the Wildlife and Countryside Act only permit a constable, on reasonable suspicion that the person is committing or has committed an offence under Part 1 of the Act, to *search an item that a suspect is using*. In trying to obtain evidence of a wildlife offence, this is of little use; the officer needs to search *for* evidence, for instance an illegal trap, a poisoned bait, a victim of poisoning etc. Furthermore, most of the items sought most likely are not *being used or even in the possession of the suspect* but *had been used or had been in the suspect's possession* – past tense. This section also includes the power to search a person.

For police officers carrying out searches this wording severely restricts searches without warrant. In some circumstances a warrant could be obtained but the time delay could be anything from a few hours to a couple of days, by which time any evidence may have been spirited away or claimed a victim.

In 2004, after much haggling by the author and a colleague with lawyers within the Scottish Executive as it was then, the wording was altered to:

Section 19.–*(1) If a constable suspects with reasonable cause that any person **is committing or has committed** an offence under this Part, the constable may without warrant–*
(a) stop and search that person if the constable suspects with reasonable cause that evidence of the commission of the offence is to be found on that person;
*(b) **search for**, search or examine any thing which that person may then be using **or may have used, or may have or have had in his possession**, if the constable suspects with reasonable cause that evidence of the commission of the offence is to be found in or on that thing;*
*(c) **arrest that person;***
(d) seize and detain for the purposes of proceedings under this Part any thing which may be evidence of the commission of the offence or may be liable to be forfeited under section 21.
*(2) If a constable suspects with reasonable cause that any person is committing **or has committed** an offence under this Part, he may, for the purpose of exercising the powers conferred by subsection (1), enter any land other than a dwelling or lockfast premises.*

These and other changes have made a remarkable difference to the success of searches in wildlife investigations in Scotland and would benefit policing in England and Wales equally well.

3. Wildlife and Countryside Act, Schedule 1A

Currently in England and Wales it is not an offence to harass a hen harrier skydancing or prospecting for a place to nest in order to make it move on from the area. There have been numerous reports from bird watchers over the years of a male harrier skydancing to encourage a mate with a view to nesting, then suddenly there is no sign of the bird or birds. Their disappearance may have been as a result of natural causes, they may have been shot or trapped, or they may have been harassed so much they have moved on. There is no offence of harassing the bird until it actually starts to nest.

The incorporation in England and Wales of Schedule 1A into the Wildlife and Countryside Act where it is an offence to recklessly or intentionally harass any wild bird in that schedule or to knowingly cause or permit any person to do so may have made a difference in some hen harrier investigations described in this book. The hen harrier would be the most obvious bird to include on the schedule, though it may be appropriate to include birds such as the goshawk, peregrine or red kite in due course.

4. Wildlife and Countryside Act – Vicarious liability

Vicarious liability, had it been available in England and Wales, may likewise have been used to good effect in some of the cases described in the chapters of this book. For a landowner or sporting agent to be convicted of *knowingly* causing or permitting an offence is almost impossible. The principal witnesses are likely to be employees and if they speak up, instead of being lauded by others in the game management industry for their integrity they are more likely to be sacked, then shunned by former colleagues. Without vicarious liability, those who could easily put an end to much of the wildlife crime described by subtly encouraging or specifically directing their employees to break the law are virtually untouchable. This will not have escaped the notice of those in the Westminster Government, hence their reluctance to incorporate it into legislation.

5. *Wildlife and Countryside Act – Snares*

Snaring legislation is woefully inadequate in England and Wales when compared with the revamped version of the same relevant section of the 1981 Act in Scotland. Wales has introduced a code of conduct but the legislation still falls short. There is no provision for stops on snares in England and Wales which prevent the captive animal being strangled or are less likely to hold animals such as dogs or deer that may be caught by a leg. There is no requirement to remove victims of snares at every inspection, making the offence of failing to check snares much more difficult to prove. There is no ban on snaring in situations where the animal may be subjected to entanglement, suspension or drowning. There is no training programme for those involved in snaring, nor registration with the police, nor mandatory tags on snares to identify the user or indeed record keeping. These requirements have made a big difference to the number of snaring complaints reported to the police in Scotland and could easily be replicated in England and Wales. Consideration of animal welfare is common sense and should be obligatory.

6. *Revocation of General Licences*

The revocation of the right to use general licences on the balance of probabilities should also be made available in England and Wales. This is the most elementary of sanctions that could be imposed on individuals or, more likely, over areas of land where there has been regular evidence of raptor persecution or abuse of the licence conditions.

SCOTLAND
Ongoing Developments

There are a number of interesting developments in the pipeline with the efforts of the Scottish Government and Police Scotland to tackle wildlife crime. Items 1 to 6 below are some of the proposed work summarised in the 2015 report *Wildlife Crime in Scotland*, which was published towards the end of 2016, with the Scottish Government making the following commitments for priority work ahead. The remaining 7 items detail work ongoing to inform on what, if any, sanctions might need to be imposed to address the continuing wildlife crime linked to game management.

1 Increase penalties

The Wildlife Crime Penalties Review Group, commissioned by the Scottish Government, published their report in November 2015. The group, chaired by Professor Mark Poustie of Strathclyde University, concentrated their work on the current wildlife crime priorities: bat persecution, badger persecution, illegal trade in endangered species, freshwater pearl mussels, poaching and raptor persecution. They recommended, *inter alia*, that penalties on summary conviction for the most serious wildlife crimes be increased to a fine of up to £40,000 and up to 12 months imprisonment. Conviction on indictment should be more commonly available to courts, with a penalty of up to five years imprisonment. If this increase is agreed by the Scottish Government it would pave the way for authority for covert surveillance by the police on private land to be more easily obtained.

2 Consider creating new sentencing guidelines

With the establishment of the Scottish Sentencing Council in October 2015, sentencing guidelines should be developed for wildlife offences to enhance the consistency and transparency of sentencing. The Council prepare sentencing guidelines for the courts, publish guideline judgements issued by the courts as well as information about sentences handed down by the court. The Council can also conduct research and provide general advice and guidance.

3 Create a new Wildlife Crime Investigation Unit

The commitment for Police Scotland to create a new Wildlife Crime Investigation Unit was noteworthy. This appears in the report as a Scottish Government commitment so can we assume that the Scottish Government, through PAW, will at least be part-funding it? Ideally (and theoretically) the unit might incorporate a sergeant in charge (or maybe even an inspector if it is taken seriously enough) and all six of the current full-time wildlife crime liaison officers.

Since the unit would be dealing with some of the more complex enquiries, particularly vicarious liability and wildlife crimes where a court might seek recovery of profit under the Proceeds of Crime Act (POCA) this would require at least one detective officer with fraud training and trained in the identification of assets for recovery. This officer may also be tasked to try to develop a means of establishing the financial value to an estate of killing protected predators, making certain crimes fit more clearly into the category of serious and organised crime. Spain already assigns a financial value to individual raptors (see later) which a person convicted of killing one has to pay in addition to any other penalty.

There are other specialist police services that would be required from time to time, such as scene of crime officers and search-trained officers but it's doubtful they would be part of this unit; more likely they would be identified with the unit and could be called on as required, as could any of another 100 or so trained wildlife crime officers.

The unit would need to have close links with the National Wildlife Crime Unit in respect of the preparation of intelligence packages. Might Police Scotland second crime analysts to the NWCU to work solely on targets in Scotland? They would also benefit from the expertise of one or more of the four NWCU investigative support officers, though again that would probably be on an ad hoc basis.

In the past there has been at least one dog in Scotland trained to sniff pesticides. This seems very risky for a dog, though the former Lothian and Borders force were impressed by what theirs could do. Drones are now used in policing and it doesn't take much imagination to think of the advantages they could bring to a wildlife crime unit, though RIP(S)A authority might be required for some of the potential uses.

Trying to obtain evidence for a prosecution in many wildlife cases will be about the biggest challenge in their investigative career for police officers. Gary Aitken, the fiscal then in charge of the Wildlife and Environmental Crime Unit, hit the nail on the head when he said, when giving evidence to the Environment, Climate Change and Land Reform Committee of the Scottish Parliament in relation to the Scottish Government Wildlife Crime Report, 2015:

> The criminal killing of wildlife species on land has been described to me as a murder investigation with a serious fraud investigation tacked on to the end of it.

Alas in times of such financial restraints the reality is that the ideal situation as described will be pared right back. Additional officers to fight wildlife crime will be minimal and, even if there is funding from the Scottish Government it will be to try to increase the effectiveness of the unit on a shoestring budget. In actual fact there is no official 'Wildlife Crime Unit' within Police Scotland, but the existing voluntary cross-divisional assistance by the full-time wildlife crime liaison officers for each other provides a reasonably effective response that also encourages learning and the sharing of experience. It also demonstrates that in a national police force the most appropriate resources can be allocated to an incident anywhere in Scotland.

Hopefully, at some stage in the future, Police Scotland will put a more official structure around the existing practices to form the Wildlife Crime Investigation Unit announced by the Scottish Government in the 2015 *Wildlife Crime in Scotland* report. Hopes were raised but back to reality. Meantime we will await an official update of any increase.

4 A review of prevention measures

This is to include a review of prevention measures to safeguard vulnerable species from illegal persecution, including through the operation of the Partnership against Wildlife Crime and in support of Police Scotland in their work to target wildlife crime hotspots. It was heartening that the Environment Secretary stated, 'We are prepared to introduce legislation where necessary'.

One of the 'hotspots' is the Cairngorms National Park and the measures are likely to include the utilisation of dedicated special constables there.

Awareness-raising should also be included under this heading. The public – and indeed those involved in various forms of land and game management– being made more aware of the types and extent of wildlife crime is both preventive and assists enforcement. Social media, in particular blogs such as Raptor Persecution UK, excel in this field. Likewise some conservation organisations, such as RSPB, plus animal welfare organisations, in particular OneKind and the League against Cruel Sports regularly publish or comment on details of wildlife crime. The police – and this is across the UK, not just in Scotland – need to step up a gear and make better use of their force websites and press releases to bring wildlife crime trends and incidents to public attention much more quickly than at present *where that does not negatively affect a live investigation*. This would give reassurance to the public that the police are serious about dealing effectively with wildlife crime and that they take the lead while other statutory and non-government organisations are there, very ably, to assist.

5 Lord Bonomy's review

Lord Bonomy's review, published in November 2016, addressed the difficulties in enforcing hunting legislation. It included a proposed Code of Practice for the conduct of hunt activities, consideration of the augmenting of the term deliberate with the term reckless, of whether vicarious liability is appropriate if an offence is committed, of extending the time limit for bringing prosecutions and of the use of independent hunt monitors.

A consultation on protecting wild mammals in Scotland was launched by the Scottish Government on 6 October 2017 and runs till 31 January 2018. Environment Secretary Roseanna Cunningham said:

> This consultation seeks to explore recommendations to improve animal welfare legislation and the contributions we receive will be of considerable value in informing our thinking. Scotland led the way in 2002 by banning the hunting of wild mammals with dogs and we remain committed to improving animal welfare across the board.

Hopefully any changes made by the Scottish Parliament to improve the enforcing of hunting legislation or other welfare issues affecting wild mammals will in due course be replicated in England and Wales.

6 Licensing of game shooting

The most difficult and high-profile wildlife crime issue to be addressed, UK-wide, is the killing of raptors, particularly on driven grouse moors.

As a prelude to tackling this problem, a review of game bird hunting and licensing in other European countries was commissioned by the Scottish Government. The results were published in mid-February 2017. It is an excellent, in-depth publication covering 14 countries but concentrating mainly on Germany, France, Sweden, Norway and Spain. These countries all license shooting (mainly referred to as 'hunting') to some degree and in every case have elements that are worthy of consideration for Scotland. The Scottish Government will hopefully manage to use the most relevant parts and create new licensing legislation that will help to solve our dreadful reputation for raptor persecution. With any luck we might manage (yet again) to show the Westminster Government how to better deal with the criminals blighting Scotland's reputation.

We already have in Scotland:

- The best wildlife legislation in the UK – although it is almost impossible to enforce it against raptor-related crime in the uplands
- Six full-time and approximately 100 part-time police officers trained to a high standard of wildlife crime investigation
- Within the Crown Office and Procurator Fiscal Service a Wildlife and Environmental Crime Unit comprising four full-time prosecutors and with access to an Advocate
- Back-up support from specialist areas of policing such as search, fraud, proceeds of crime confiscation
- Back-up support from a number of government organisations, especially in forensics and chemical analysis
- Back-up support and advice from many non-government organisations
- The possibility of sanctions such as clawing back often substantial single farm payments, though the situations in which this can be used with success have been dramatically eroded since its inception

- The possibility of revocation of general licences.
- Reasonable penalties, with the strong likelihood of an increase that would be adequate to deal with a landowner or sporting agent who indulged in raptor persecution to improve profits from shooting
- Vicarious liability
- The availability of common law crimes such as culpable and reckless conduct and conspiracy under which to consider a prosecution for the most serious of wildlife crimes
- The ability of the chief constable to revoke firearm and shotgun certificates where the holder is no longer considered suitable to hold or use firearms

Most other countries have an individual hunting licence system. We have tried that already in the UK in the form of a game licence, and it was scrapped some years ago. In any case hopefully the Scottish Government should be considering the loss of the right to shoot on a particular piece of land as well as the loss of the right of an individual to shoot.

So what we need from this game shooting licensing review is a sanction that will stop landowners and sporting agents in their tracks from directing, encouraging or turning a blind eye to raptor-related crime. The landowners, whether they be addressed as Lord, Lady, Sir or just plain Mr or Mrs are the key to this problem of killing birds of prey. If they *really* want it stopped in case they risk going to jail or the suspension of the right for shooting to take place on their land then they will most certainly devise a means to ensure their employees comply with their instructions.

The European Commission has called for 'well-regulated hunting' with, amongst other conditions, full compliance with the law. They correctly state that 'management aimed at raising artificially high yields of one species can be detrimental, particularly if it is linked to illegal persecution of birds of prey'. Most other countries have encouraged their hunters to be, in addition, conservationists.

Phrases are used in other countries such as 'long-term balance to be achieved between man and the environment'. If game management plans were to be adopted here, as they are in some other countries, they could specify measures for the improvement of habitats as agreed possibly between SNH and landowners; that they must not merely focus only on game species but must produce a balanced plan that will also benefit a large number of protected species.

It was interested to read that: 'research commissioned by the French National Hunting Federation in 2014 found that 48% of hunters are involved in conservation volunteering and a hunter spends an average of 75 hours a year volunteering (which amounts to an annual contribution of 78 million hours per year). This was calculated to be equivalent to 1.6 billion EUR (gross) contribution to the economy and to represent the equivalent contribution of more than 50,000 full time jobs. The same study concluded hunting contributes more than 3.6 billion EUR per annum to the French economy as a whole'.

The Spanish Experience

Reading the outcome of the commissioned report, Spain is possibly nearest to the UK in terms of private land ownership, game shooting and raptor persecution. As in this country it is permissible for the owner of land to hunt the game on his/her land, but the game itself does not belong to the landowner. Rather, it is regarded as a natural resource belonging to the country as a whole. The principal difference is that in Spain they have in recent years been investing in an EU-funded project to address this criminality and to quote the report: 'The illegal killing of raptors in Spain is now decreasing following the success of the Life+ VENENO project to tackle the problem through *effective enforcement and sanctions*'. The report continued: 'SEO/ Birdlife, the non-governmental Spanish ornithological society, worked with the Spanish environmental police and regional authorities on the EU funded Life+ project to respond to the problem of raptor persecution. Investment was made to provide specifically trained officers in the police force to work with NGOs and to raise public awareness of the unacceptability of wildlife poisoning. The public were further engaged by the provision of a freephone reporting line and the development of legal precedents for attaching an individual monetary value to birds killed illegally, based on the public interest and the level of public investment in protecting the particular species'.

The report went on: 'The Life+ VENENO project brought about the establishment of legal precedents on sanctions. It also developed good practice on cooperation between police and environmental bodies, training officers to gather evidence of poisoning and working together to carry this out on the ground, with the help of canine units. More than thirty prosecutions were successfully brought under the project. In 2007 the maximum fine for bird crime was increased to 2 million EUR. The Criminal Code enacts sentences of imprisonment ranging from four months to two years, disqualification from a profession or occupation and disqualification from exercising the right to hunt or fish for a period of two to four years. These sanctions are used concurrently and the Spanish bird conservation body consider this layering of sanctions as vital to the effectiveness of the approach'.

Sadly, if like Spain, EU funding is required for projects like this, there will be less chance of replicating the Spanish approach in either Scotland or the UK in the future.

As in Scotland, in some regions of Spain there are also provisions within Spanish Law to hold landowners or tenants of land vicariously responsible for wildlife crime which takes place on their land. Possible penalties range from 25,000 to 100,000 EUR plus the possibility of total or partial suspension of hunting on the land where the offence has taken place for a term ranging from six months to two years.

As an example of penalty, in October 2015 a farmer was convicted of laying out nine poisoned baits, poisoning six Spanish

Imperial eagles and a fox. His crimes were uncovered with the assistance of canine units used to search his land. He was sentenced to 18 months' imprisonment, a three-year disqualification from hunting following release from prison and a fine of 360,000 EUR (then £259,800) to be paid to the regional government for the estimated value of the six eagles.

Some years ago the author spent a week on a course run by the Spanish police, which hosted one wildlife or environmental crime officer from each constituent country of the EU. The situation in Spain, even at that time, was that police officers in the Service of Nature Protection of the Civil Guard (SEPRONA) had an amazing amount of equipment at their disposal not only to investigate wildlife crime but to check air, water and soil quality. In effect they were combining the equivalent of the jobs in Scotland of Police Scotland and Scottish Environment Protection Agency. They were most certainly in the lead on wildlife crime investigation in Europe (and this still seems to be the case) followed by the UK, Germany and Sweden.

Evidence to the Scottish Parliament's Environment, Climate Change and Land Reform (CCLR) Committee

In May 2017, after hearing evidence regarding the review of game bird hunting and licensing, and debating the need or otherwise for licensing of game shooting, the Scottish Parliament's Environment, Climate Change and Land Reform (CCLR) Committee reported to the Cabinet Secretary for Environment, Climate Change and Land Reform in the following terms:

The Committee recommends the Scottish Government explore with stakeholders the need for and benefit of such a licensing system, how it might operate in practice, what it might encompass, how it could be appropriately enforced and whether such a system might feasibly be trialled in a specific area.

SCOTTISH GOVERNMENT
proposed measures

On 31 May 2017, after having received a lengthy scientific report from SNH that reviewed the disappearance of satellite-tagged golden eagles and clearly after having taken all the other evidence of criminal acts against raptors into consideration, the Environment Secretary announced the following series of measures to be put in place:

Environmental impact of grouse moors

Set up an independently-led group to look at the environmental impact of grouse moor management practices. (This group is in progress though, in November 2017, has not yet reported back).

These would include muirburn, the use of medicated grit and mountain hare culls, and to recommend options for regulation including licensing and other measures which could be put in place without new primary legislation.

Geographical area of concern for wildlife crime

Immediately review all available legal measures which could be used to target geographical areas of concern. Increase resources for the detection and investigation of wildlife crime and work with Police Scotland to pilot the use of special constables in the Cairngorms National Park.

An SNH report identified hotspots in which tagged eagles completely disappeared. Could a licence have the condition that spot checks on licensed estates, particularly of their traps and snares, be carried out by the police? This would allow the police to 'target geographical areas of concern'. Bearing in mind the need for corroboration, this would be an ideal use for special constables acting along with a regular officer, which doesn't have to be restricted to the Cairngorms National Park.

The report showed that over 40 satellite-tagged golden eagles had disappeared in suspicious circumstances in a 12-year period. There must also be a corresponding proportion of eagles that were not tagged that met the same fate. That outcome can also be extended to hen harriers in the hen harrier satellite-tagging programme, and to goshawks and several other birds of prey which are not meantime sat-tagged. Grouse management is no longer able to hide behind lame excuses and barefaced lies.

Licensing – at least of grouse moors – seems inevitable. Withdrawing a licence from an individual would have little effect: that individual could be sacked and replaced. The licence would need to be withdrawn in relation to land, for example a whole grouse moor. Simply withdrawing the right to shoot over the land would hit landowners hard in their deep pockets but would that be enough? Depending on the length of any licence withdrawal, if they were still able to continue land 'management' for grouse in preparation for the reinstatement of their licence they could still burn heather, including rank heather suitable for nesting hen harriers. They could also continue predator control, which on some moors would leave raptors and some protected mammals at the same level of risk as before. Whether a licence could be tailored to permit (or in the case of withdrawal, to ban) identified activities related to game management would be a decision for Scottish Government.

It has been obvious for years in Scotland and the north of England that driven grouse moors under the same management employ the same predator control tactics. It is much more than coincidence that these estates are the ones on which crime against raptors and other protected species is most prevalent. It would be a major crime reduction factor if a licence were to be revoked in relation to one estate, that the licences be revoked for all estates under the same management.

SSPCA Powers

Rule out giving the Scottish SPCA more investigative powers, in light of legal advice.

For reasons given earlier increasing the powers of the SSPCA was never going to work. The SSPCA do an excellent job with animal welfare and not taking on additional work with wildlife crime will allow them to concentrate more on serious animal welfare issues, puppy farming and dog fighting in particular.

The Gamekeepers' Role

Examine how best to protect the valuable role of gamekeepers in rural Scotland.

There are many gamekeepers who do indeed carry out a valuable role and they deserve some credit and support. They have been operating in the dark shadow of the criminals in their midst for years and it is unfair to group them with the landowners, sporting agents and gamekeepers who have brought their occupation to the dreadful situation in which it is now immersed. This measure no doubt stems from Ms Cunningham's comment,

> The continued killing of protected species of birds of prey damages the reputation of law-abiding gamekeepers, landowners and indeed the country as a whole. Those who carry out these crimes do so in defiance of the will of Parliament, the people, and their own peers. That must end.

It is interesting that she has omitted 'law-abiding sporting agents.' Was that intentional or was it a mistake?

How the Scottish Government would protect the gamekeepers' role could be difficult to determine but many of them certainly do not warrant being lumped in with their criminal colleagues. The land on which they operate may in the future be subject to licensing but apart from the stipulations licensing may bring, the gamekeepers should have nothing to fear from the police or any other authority unless they are involved in criminal activity.

Gamekeepers are best placed to pass on information to the police about illegal practices being committed by their peers, yet they rarely do so. The same applies to landowners and their respective associations, who must be well aware of which landowners and sporting agents encourage, or in some cases order, their employees to commit illegal practices. Had they grasped the nettle and reported these matters the game shooting industry would not be in the calamitous state that it now finds itself.

Shooting Estates' Effect on Economy and Biodiversity

Commission research into the costs and benefits of large shooting estates to Scotland's economy and biodiversity

This measure is interesting in view of the many detriments (rather than benefits) some – though certainly not all – of the large shooting estates have foisted upon Scotland. Though there is no update by November 2017 it'll be interested to read, in due course, how much these estates cost the public purse in subsidies and how better use may be made of the subsidies and some of the land.

Land Registry and Shooting Estates

Also relevant to game shooting is the intention of parliament, during 2017, to look at the ownership and management of estates and hopefully ensure these details are included in a land register. In any other business this would equate to a chain of command. This needs to be done as a matter of urgency so that in vicarious liability cases the specific individual who is liable for activity on an estate can be identified and reported for prosecution.

*

Wildlife crime, particularly that occurring on intensively managed driven grouse moors, is under the spotlight as never before. As has been evidenced by the accounts of a fraction of the known criminality that has taken place over the past few years it unfortunately remains part and parcel of much of our uplands, carried out by servants on behalf of their masters. The number of crimes against raptors and some other protected wildlife in the north of England, and the south and east of Scotland is nothing short of a disgrace, indeed a national disgrace. A landowner or sporting agent being convicted and receiving a substantial jail sentence is the factor, at least in the meantime, that would make the biggest difference. Thankfully, at the end of 2017, the British Association for Shooting and Conservation has gone further than any other of the land and game management organisations, stating that killing raptors to protect game birds was a 'fool's bargain'. With 74% of convictions for raptor persecution in the last 25 years being against gamekeepers and other game interests surely the other organisations will stop burying their heads in the sand.

We have accomplished many improvements already in Scotland but there remains scope for expansion, adaptation and creativity. Some exciting ideas and processes are in progress, at least in Scotland. The availability of increased sentences on conviction may clear the way for the police to carry our surveillance on 'private' land more easily, and there seems little doubt that the licensing of driven grouse shooting will take place relatively soon. Reviews underway may indeed conclude that there are more economically viable ways of managing (and subsidising) our uplands for public benefit, while still providing at least the same level of employment. It would be fantastic to have a snapshot of the use of the present burnt, treeless and manicured moorlands a few decades from now.